Babbling Echoes

Soundings from Yesteryear

H. A. Dorfman

Hamilton Books
A member of
The Rowman & Littlefield Publishing Group
Lanham • Boulder • New York • Toronto • Plymouth, UK

British Library Cataloging in Publication Information Available

Library of Congress Control Number: 2012942548
ISBN: 978-0-7618-5927-7

"Coffee Cutoff Causes Chaos" reprinted with permission of The Boston Herald.

"That tuneful nymph, the babbling echo,
who has not learned to conceal what
is told her, nor yet is able to speak
until another speaks."

Ovid

Contents

Introduction

Five years after moving with my family from Commack, New York, to Manchester, Vermont, I began my first 'formal' writing. (I got *paid* for it.) I do not consider the writing I did at night at the Suffolk County branch of *Newsday*, on Long Island, where I was a stringer covering high school sports, to be very 'formal.' The pay was in line with the informality.

But in 1973, I began to do what I'd always wanted to do: write whatever I pleased.

What is it that provoked me to revisit the file of my newspaper columns and articles, written in the 1970's and 1980's? Some inner yearning? A gnawing boredom? I'm not sure. But that experience further provoked the thought of putting a few of my favorites, long buried in an album my wife Anita had made, between the covers of a real book. For what purpose?

James Reston said of his writing, "If it's far away, it's news, but if it's close at home, it's sociology." The subjects I wrote about in my columns those many years ago were all 'close at home.' So maybe I wish now to compile a book of sociology, stuff that, perhaps, can still be of interest to a reader or two. In any case, the articles interest me—or, more correctly, they allow me to recall some events and thoughts that put a smile in my heart. They produce sounds that echo through my memory and do not fade.

So I decided to keep them around. Listen to them again. And record them, for my own self-indulgence and, perhaps, for the pleasure of others.

I believe the columns included in the book can, for the most part, speak for themselves. But they are dated, after all, and therefore require some short introduction. These brief commentaries (a couple, not-so-brief) will, I hope, illuminate for the reader the paths that led to the columns' origins—an explanation, so to speak, of circumstances and/or whimsy at the time of their birth.

Some 'postscripts,' I felt, were also necessary. Bringing some matters written about in the past up-to-date with current information and illuminating remarks.

About the format: I decided it was easiest (for me) to have the columns and articles presented chronologically, coming across these pages in the same order they were originally published.

Finally, I have taken the liberty of making a few changes—not in content, although I was sorely tempted. I've taken these few editorial liberties (after all, I wrote this stuff), by changing or correcting words that were either carelessly type-set or stupidly conceived. (I have probably introduced some others.) Some punctuation was changed—and I made a few syntax adjustments, attempting to make the experience easier for the reader—at least in that regard.

Fifty articles appear. A round number and a manageable one, for writer and, I hope, for reader.

H.A. Dorfman
2011

1

Edmund and the Birds

Upland Winter, January–February, 1973

My wife, Anita, our two young children and I moved from Commack, New York, to Manchester, Vermont, during the summer of 1968. I was hired to teach literature to junior high school kids. Anita, Melissa, Danny and I lived up a dirt road—isolated, yet only three miles from town. We loved it there.

One of the reasons our family moved to Vermont was my desire to have the time to write. The time? The salary a Vermont school teacher brought home (much reduced from the one I earned on Long Island) could afford me (us) no such luxury.

I was a regular moon-lighter, tending bar a few nights a week. I also moved confounding—and heavy—pieces of furniture and collectibles for antique sellers at their shows. I umpired high school and college baseball games. Anything that could bring in a few bucks.

But I somehow did manage to find periods of time for occasional writing. I referred to The Writer's Market *regularly, looking for some magazine willing to publish my freelance work. I should mention: that work was all non-fiction. I'd made one attempt at fiction. No one read it but me. It was an embarrassment—especially to someone who taught Mann and Melville, Kafka and Conrad, Dostoyevsky and Austen each day. I knew great fiction writing, and mine was not close to qualifying as 'good.'*

In 1971, my first magazine article was published. Home Life, *a Southern Baptist publication printed "Helping a Boy Grow"—an over-written and somewhat didactic how-to-be-a-good-father-to-a-son piece. The following year* Baseball Digest *published my article about under-appreciated major league players, in this case, second basemen.*

I've read that Hemingway papered his walls with rejection slips. I could have papered Grand Central Station. It was time for a new approach. I decided on writing for newspapers. Edmund is included in this book because it was my 'breakthrough.' A frivolous piece, accepted by a paper that was published seasonally—actually six times a year.

They were looking for something about birds. What did a guy brought up in New York City know about birds? Speaking for myself: nothing. "Can I focus on a cat while including birds?" I asked. I got the go-ahead. Go ahead for what?

But being a Vermonter now, living in the woods, a birdfeeder hanging outside our family room window, I tried to rise to the occasion. I'm not quite sure how far off the ground I got with this piece. But it was accepted—and it led me to believe that journalism was for me. Even (especially?) frivolous writing.

Soon after this article appeared, I began writing a column for The Manchester Journal, *a local weekly. But "Edmund . . ." was the first of hundreds to follow—and, probably, that is all I can think of to justify its inclusion.*

I had never fostered a wish to become involved with a cat. But there is a wide chasm between wishes and powers.

My two youngsters merely held a kitten, loved it immediately and were told by the owner that it was available upon consent of their parents, both present at the time. Mother, kitten-smitten herself, tactfully pretended not to have heard the offer; father froze, thereby forfeiting his chance to cast a negative vote. The kitten was ours.

The little animal and I established a mutual indifference. I found kitty to be mannerly and remarkably discreet in his personal habits. We did not need each other but acted with civility and respect whenever our paths happened to cross.

I can even admit to having developed a somewhat positive attitude toward our new pet. We'd recently moved to the Green Mountains of Vermont. Our house was set in the middle of woods active with wildlife. "A place for everything, everything in its place." But the field mice didn't seem to know their place very well, and I viewed kitty as a potential teaching instrument for these confused and disrespectful rodents.

As time passed, the cat, Edmund, became an enthusiastic and accomplished mouser. Order reigned in this humble home and its surrounding wood—for a short while, at least. Edmund then discovered birds.

His enthusiasm, dexterity and activity became more evident daily. Edmund had learned to find his own way in the world. This in itself did not alarm anyone.

Each morning, however, we began to find beautiful winged creatures (so rare to former city dwellers) lying in non-resplendent fashion on our doorstep. Chickadees, phoebes, bluejays, nuthatches! Edmund's deliveries were more reliable than the milkman's. My wife grew more upset each morning. I was bewildered. And then, the feather that broke the bird-watcher's back: "Aaaarghh, a scarlet tanager," cried my wife.

That did it.

"We've got to do something," she said.

The remainder of my morning was spent in the local library, surrounded by piles of books, the number 636.8 stamped on their bindings. I flipped pages desperately, searching for a solution to the cat-bird issue. Suddenly, the answer appeared at hand: "Chapter Six: TEACHING CATS NOT TO KILL BIRDS."

But Chapter Six was not at all encouraging. It told of an old ornithologist who had received 305 letters from people who were convinced of the impossibility of teaching cats to refrain from their bird-stalking activities.

Seventy-two other letter writers claimed that cats most certainly *could* be trained not to kill birds. Of course, of the seventy-two—thirty-seven apparent bird-lovers—most said whipping the cat would turn the trick. Eight apparent cat-lovers said a scolding would be quite sufficient. However, there were other more original and ingenious responses.

Nine 'experts' claimed that tying the dead bird around the cat's neck would prove to be a successful deterrent; one suggested drenching the cat with water. So much for the cat.

The remaining responses were bird-centered. Two suggested that pepper, poured liberally over the dead bird, would work wonders. The final authority advised that kerosene must be added to the pepper. ("Better safe than sorry," his motto.)

Fortunately, the writers of the book agreed with none of these procedures. But I found their solution to be a bit beyond the limits of my personality and skill, to say nothing of my credulity.

The authors' directions were quite complete—too complete for me. I must convince cat not to be jealous of bird, because I love them both! Show cat that the birds are our friends! It was too formidable a task to finish reading the entire set of instructions. So I did not.

Hopelessly, I returned to the other 636.8's. Almost immediately I found in another book, "Cats and Our Feathered Friends." The teaching was simple, it said.

Get a caged bird, and watch the cat sharply. Wait until the cat notices the bird and crouches for the attack. Then, open fire on fearless feline with a water pistol or peashooter. But wait! Under no circumstance is the cat to see you doing this to him. He must believe that the *bird* is responsible for the outrage.

It was all there in the book. Again, I could not go on.

I placed sixteen books about cats back into their Dewey Decimals, made a courageous decision, checked out one book, put it under my arm and left the library trying to effect a Humphrey Bogart tone, repeating to myself, "No, pussy, you must not hurt the nice little birdie."

I read in Chapter Six all the how-to-do's and what-to-say's to be employed during the development of Edmund's bird-loving attitude. What degradation!

However, the opportunity to begin was ever-present, with Edmund bringing in a record catch each day. My first demand was addressed to the family. Top security. No one was to witness the cat's basic training (or the trainer's basic debasement).

This demand made, I awaited the dreaded moment of confrontation, which came when Edmund presented his next bird. I sounded a warning to clear the area and went into my act. I baby-talked the cat; I suffered; I followed every directive the book provided. Edmund surely thought me a fool. I put him down. He dropped the bird at my feet and disappeared into the woods. Lesson one had ended.

Humiliation was replaced by fear—of having been spied upon. It was justified: my little boy tipped his hand at bedtime with, "Good night, Doctor Doolittle."

My work with cat seemed to show results, for Edmund was bringing home fewer birds and had ceased his sentry beneath the feeder. He apparently had chosen to respond, if at his own leisurely rate.

Yet I could not help suspecting that he was far too intelligent an animal to have succumbed to my pseudo-professionalism. He had made me suffer through two weeks of intensive training and had then probably tired of the game. The fact remained that there were no more bird deliveries from Edmund. He had let me off the hook.

My wife assures me that patience, skill and love (though feigned) won over the cat. I think not. When Edmund and I are alone together, a half-Cheshire smirk appears on his whiskered countenance.

At any rate, the birds seem easier on the wing, my wife is ecstatic, and, on occasion, the children are permitted to address me as Doctor Doolittle without fear of reprisal.

2

A Labor Day Revisited

The Manchester Journal, August 30, 1973

A few years after having moved to Vermont, I began a weekly column for the local news-paper. Sitting and reflecting, days before Labor Day, '73, I wondered what to write about. I recalled a Labor Day five years previous. I had an experience that involved two ladies I loved very much: my older sisters, Dolly and Anita (not a typo; two Anitas in the family).

Neither sister had ever played golf before. Years later, Dolly became a champion at her golf club. Sister Anita played once. "More than enough," she said. For some unexplain-able reason they chose to initiate themselves on the busiest weekend of the summer. I had not been informed / consulted. My summer job (I taught when school was in session) was as a ranger on a golf course. The golf course in Commack, New York—where they chose to play.

After five years in Vermont I believe myself to once more be sound in mind, as well as in body. Urban upset, suburban psychosis—all this seems part of the distant past.

My tonic has been the tranquility of Manchester living. Now I can even talk of traumatic times which were responsible for my broken spirit, such as the Labor Day experience on a Long Island golf course.

I happened to be working at the course that summer; my position was triflingly termed "handyman." A short tenure was all that was required to prove that neither miscellany nor handiness were in my bag. But the administrators of the course did perceive one talent in me. I could navigate an electric cart while reading a book. So they demoted me to full-time golf course ranger. (Some disparagingly referred to my cart as "The Bookmobile.")

The new job was perfect. I sped around the course each day like a soldier of for-tune, waiting to confront potentially dangerous situations, my intervention changing chaos into calm—harassment into harmony. I waited, but mostly I just drove around and read.

Then came Labor Day. The heat was without mercy; golfers were everywhere. Play was maddeningly slow. Temperaments began to match the discomfort index. People were being struck by stray balls hit by golfers whose patience had broken.

The layout of the third hole had been changed only a few days earlier, adding confusion and more delay to an already intolerable situation. By two o'clock in the afternoon all was unwell. Chaos and harassment reigned without fear of overthrow.

At this time, the realization came to me that my worth had sunk to its lowest ebb. It seemed to me that even the most adroit golf course ranger in the hemisphere would have lost control of this super-saturation of humidity, perspiration, frustration, and ill-will. My assessment produced accompanying feelings of defeat, which were responsible for my next act.

Adjoining the 18-hole golf course was a nine-hole, par-three course. Play on this small course was usually quite light—mostly neophytes, self-conscious women and cardiac cases at play. It, too, was part of my domain, but it needed a ranger's attention no more than it needed a drought. In the past I had driven over it only when short-cutting back to the clubhouse. Suddenly it occurred to me that here was the haven where my sanity and self-respect might be preserved.

I sped toward this oasis, dodging golfers, clubs and balls, my books bouncing on the seat beside me, symbols of my worth. I bumped along through the wooded area between the two courses and suddenly bolted into the clearing which was the seventh fairway of the par-three course. What greeted me was appalling, far worse than what I was fleeing from. I'd fled toward Elysium only to find myself up the Stygian Creek.

The small course was swarming with bodies. The population per square yard defied statistical hyperbole. I went into a state of shock. Then I looked toward the seventh tee, and my shock was compounded. There, on and near the tee, were thirteen—a baking baker's dozen—people in a variety of sizes, shapes, sexes and colors, milling around with a collective attitude of sweeping disgust. Seeing me, they grew animated and began waving their arms, shouting to me and pointing toward the green.

I still was in somewhat of a traumatic state, but the group's excitement began to affect me. I started to drive toward them, and as I approached was able to understand their cries and grunts of anguish. I reached them; their crisis became mine. I could not escape it.

I looked toward the green, on which stood two women with golf clubs. To further describe their activities is unthinkable. Language and memory cannot adequately serve me in this connection. Though dazed once more, I was still aware of what the heat-maddened army of players stacked up at the tee expected of me. Their belief in heroics produced their hero. Without an utterance, I performed a wheelie with my golf cart and sped toward the violators of every established rule of golfing etiquette and procedure. (The women claimed afterward to have been forewarned of my approach by a wild "Hi ho Silver, away!")

They were undoubtedly hurt by what took place when I arrived upon their scene. I must admit to an inability, once again, to recall the confrontation coherently. The awful fact was that they were my sisters. Both in their 40's, neither had set foot on a golf course before. (Why they chose that day has never been discussed.) The whole thing was bizarre.

They later claimed I first addressed Thomas Paine in prayer and muttered of the times that try men's souls. "Get in the damn cart," I do remember saying. Cheers could be heard coming from the seventh tee as the three of us sped toward the clubhouse. One sister cried, the other denied. I choked accusations and expletives en route. (They say I spoke of the problems of senility.)

I resigned quietly the next afternoon, much to the surprise of the management. I told them I was allergic to grass.

Come the third of September I intend to celebrate the tenth anniversary of that infamous day by taking a prolonged walk on the beautiful, vast, serene Equinox Golf Course. It will be the first time in these ten years that I've gone near a course on Labor Day. A testimony to Vermont living. I may even bring my clubs.

3

Theo North:
Scourge of Christmas Past

The Bennington Banner, January 5, 1974

While serving drinks at a private cocktail party, I met an editor, of sorts, at The Bennington Banner, *another state newspaper, though not nearly as formidable as* The Rutland Herald. *The fellow was quite likable, and after chatting a bit, he encouraged me to write something for his newspaper: a book review. I do not like writing book reviews. Critics, Saul Bellow said, are like "deaf piano tuners."*

But I did want to introduce myself to the Banner. *I thought I could figure out a way to get around my reluctance and at the same time satisfy his need. I'm not so sure I managed it well, but I'm not going to be a critic of my own work either, so the reader is left to decide.*

DO NOT be misled: this is not a book review. There is a feeling of malevolence in my heart for paid critics in general, and I do not wish to become one of their number. Some introductory explanation is therefore in order.

Birthdays, parent days, Christmas days or any other significant occasions which warrant gift-giving thereby warrant book-giving in our family. Aside from the fact that this little tradition is pleasurable in itself, I benefit additionally because of a wife who possesses an uncanny ability to make selections based on an apparent extra-sensory perception. Her past record has been impeccable. This year, however, the inevitable happened.

If destiny took its course, I must at least confess to being the *primum mobile*. Simply, this is what it's all about.

I had the misfortune of being drawn (by the demon of bibliophiles) into the local bookstore the week before Christmas. Fifteen minutes of browsing should have been satiating, but the demon (I seem to be transferring the blame again) struck once more. Thornton Wilder's latest, *Theophilus North* was spotted, handled, charged, bagged and tucked under my arm.

I had been silently looking forward to reading Wilder's book since hearing of its publication. His works have generally entertained me and are often nourishing to the mind, though I still must admit to boredom whenever recalling *The Bridge of San Luis Rey*. (Former students of mine would consider this to be understated.) *The Eighth Day*, on the other hand, I considered to be a goody. It's been seven years since that book made its initial appearance, and my anticipation of Mr. Wilder's next book, and perhaps his last, undoubtedly made me expect too much. But I digress.

My arrival at home was not very typical. Anita glared at the familiar green bag under my arm with terror and resentment in her eyes.

"What's in there?"

"A book."

"I know. Let me see."

"Here."

"(Censored.)"

A gulp from me.

"How dare you buy a book for yourself the week before Christmas?" (Emphasis on 'before'—and, come to think of it, 'dare.')

I returned my copy of *Theophilus North* with apologies to Anita. (No need to apologize to the bookstore proprietor; he suggested a fine substitute—at greater cost.)

I certainly had something to look forward to. Pre-Christmas week was spent with the bookseller's recommended volume (Auden's *Forethoughts and Afterthoughts*, which I loved). Christmas day welcomed again—Theo North.

That is the introductory explanation.

The experience was a calamity of retribution I suppose. An almost total disappointment. The character Theophilus (call me Teddy) and his exploits in nine-layered Newport, Rhode Island, during the 1920's strained my credulity more than somewhat. (More understatement.)

Basically—(I am being intractable and snotty I fear: Teddy would attribute this behavior to excessive frustration compounded by an inferiority complex. Who knows?) Basically, I was saying, Teddy North comes off (certainly not on) as a combination of a ten-year-old Sigmund Freud, a Lone Ranger on bicycle, a Caucasian Charlie Chan, a homely Frank Merriwell, A Man from Glad *sans* gladness, a Goody Two-Shoes *sans* curls and a polylingual Elmer Fudd.

It is this Super-Teddy who provides an eminent brain surgeon with some professional food for the doctor's own gray matter; who gets an insensitive wife off her World War I flying ace husband's anatomical rear rudder; who cures an unhappy young girl's malady with a lightning-handed touch; who graciously and, yes, surreptitiously plays stud for a frustrated mother-in-waiting.

Forgive me, dear reader. You see, I am no longer able to proceed with—(good grief, I'm sounding like Teddy).

Well, that's it. Wilder is usually a master story-teller, but this one got out of hand. The language is stilted and, while a couple of characters are moving and real, too many are not—particularly the first-person narrator, T. North, who takes his place in my mind as one of the most didactic and lifeless good fellows between two book covers.

Many writers have looked back on their early years as the source of what often becomes autobiographical fiction. This appears to be what Wilder has tried to do. References to the narrator's journal, the era treated and the closing reference to Teddy's prospects of becoming a writer make this hypothesis supportable. Stronger hints are also to be found.

Saul Bellow did so well with his *Adventures of Augie March*. Michener handled it wonderfully in *The Fires of Spring*. It didn't happen here for Thornton Wilder.

My wife is not addicted to reading all my presents. She is noted for her charitable criticism of most everyone's writing (relatives included). At infrequent times of un-certainty, which occur during these reading experiences, I am consulted for the purpose of clarification or explanation. (Good for the ego when answers are available.)

She is currently reading "T.N." and has just reached page six. Already her first question has been articulated: "Is this guy kidding?"

A shrug of my shoulders was my only response.

4

Good News for Mankind

The Manchester Journal, March 14, 1974

Always searching for mankind's more positive possibilities, whatever they may be, I came across a report from a group of scientists who had recently convened at their annual convention.

Evolutionists have told man that he is a descendant of the apes; Greek writer Nikos Kazantzakis said that God makes us grubs; Mark Twain believed man's closest kin to have been the jackass. But finally—good news. Some scientists have just suggested that there are supportable comparisons to be made between early man and the wolf rather than between early man and apes, grubs, jackasses and, yes, even llamas.

The suggestion comes from an extensive report presented at the annual convention of the American Association for the Advancement of Science, held in San Francisco on March 1.

The key to all this, it seems to me, is that the scientists are talking about similarities between wolves and EARLY man. I'll listen to that kind of talk. But contemporary man? Well, Darwin and Twain seem to have stronger arguments in that regard. You see, these biologists, ethnologists, *et. al.* in San Francisco have described the wolf as a gentle, loving and sensitive animal who depends for his survival on a cooperative, supportive society. Is that you out there, contemporary man?

Now how did the "big, bad wolf" acquire such a poor and apparently unwarranted reputation? "From the media," I hear you screaming. Man's media. And, goodness, just look in man's dictionary: "WOLF, n. Slang. A man given to avid amatory pursuit of women.—v. To eat voraciously: 'wolfed down the hamburger.'" But now maybe things are turning around for the wolf and his image—and surely it will be man who will benefit from the intense study of that animal. (Put your money on the men in white smocks.)

Twenty of them (timber wolves and red wolves, that is; not white smockers) have been studied for almost three years at the Bio-Social Research Center at the University of Oregon. They are almost constantly observed as they live behind fences on three acres of land "with a forest, an apple orchard, grassy field and broad stream" (everything a man could ask for, with the exception of television, alcohol and chewing tobacco).

Dr. Fentress, director of the Center's study, says, "Their lives are natural, except that they do not eat caribou and moose, which wild wolves prefer, but dog chow and chicken." (This dietary adaptability is the one parallel between wolf and contemporary man. Speaking personally, I prefer lobster and beef steak to caribou and moose, but, except when dining out, I usually settle for the same fare the wolf enjoys at the U. of Oregon.)

Most significant in the study however, is the fact that wolves have elaborate vocal systems and can subtly coordinate with and adjust to the "moods" of men and fellow wolves. They are "obviously very finely in tune with each other" and devote much time to "being friendly, nice and reassuring to each other." Dr. Fentress has decided that wolves are "exceedingly friendly and tend to be far more subtle and sensitive than dogs." (More on dogs next week.)

Ambrose Bierce once defined MAN as an animal so lost in rapturous contemplation of what he thinks he is, that he overlooks what he indubitably ought to be. (Ambrose never wore a white smock.) Maybe, after all the searching and conjecturing (scientific and otherwise), our newly discovered brother wolf will provide the self-image we seek.

Good news for mankind; no comment from wolfkind.

Postscript—Funny thing, I haven't heard any follow-up on the scientists' theories since this article was written.

5

Youth Revisited, or, Victory for Milton and Friends

The New York Times, April, 21, 1974

On a whim, I sent a light-hearted piece to The New York Times. *The inside (second) page of their Sunday Sports Section was set aside for 'outsiders'—a sort of Op-Ed page for freelance writers or just folks who had something they wanted to say related to sport. A couple of such pieces appeared on the page each week. I was ecstatic to have this one accepted and printed. In the years that followed, ten or so more were published there. All were in some way related to baseball. My editor at the paper, Frank Litsky, was very enthusiastic about what he called my sport-specific "expertise." He said nothing about my sense of humor.*

Baseball season has been launched. That's probably why my seven-year-old's benevolent aunt presented him with a game glowingly described as a "superior baseball game for fans of all ages."

At his age, I had every major league roster written indelibly in a mind with eyes (ears, nose and throat) for the national pastime and nothing else. Then again, I was brought up in the shadow of the Polo Grounds. Vermont's Equinox Mountain provides a different type of umbrage.

Anyhow, I wasn't looking forward to cracking open the game. It would require teaching the boy the fundamentals of baseball—a bit too subtle for a youngster who's a collector of stones, wood scraps and anything that moves—or used to.

Now don't get me wrong. I love to play with the little guy, but quiet indoor strategy games were not for him.

For reasons not revealed, he said he wanted to learn this game and play it with me. I put it off. He kept after me, so we finally sat down at the kitchen table with six dodecahedrons (12-sided dice), a professional scorebook, strategy cards, a box of pretzels and two aspirins.

13

The basic rules of the game were covered in thirteen minutes. Baseball terminology and strategy took seventy-seven minutes, plus the pretzels and aspirin.

We were ready to select the teams we would manage. I became animated, and visions of youth returned. I was ten years old, leaping into the aisle of the Polo Grounds' left-field grandstand, catching the home run hit by Ernie Lombardi.

"I'll be the 1945 Giants," I announced.

Danny looked uncertain.

"What's that?" he asked.

"What team are you going to be, the Mets?"

"I'm going to be my friends."

"What?"

"It says on that book you're holding—you can be whatever team you want. I'm going to be my friends."

I didn't comment. I entered that glorious Giants line-up into the scorebook:

Hausman, 2nd base
Rucker, center field
Ott, right field
Lombardi, catcher
Gardella, left field
Weintraub, 1st base
Reyes, 3rd base
Kerr, shortstop
Voiselle, pitcher

We were ready for anybody.

"O.K., give me your lineup," I said, almost sneering.

"Steven, Jimmy, Robert ..."

"Wait a minute. What are their last names?"

He knew only a couple.

"Frankie, Aaron, Mel (his sister!), Adin, Danny (I figured he was going to be a player-manager like Ott), and Milton."

"Milton! Who's Milton?"

He briefed me on his new friend.

Bill Voiselle pitching against Milton. The first four innings were scoreless.

Nothing much happened—his team youthfully inept, mine rusty after an almost thirty-year layoff.

Milton had a wild spell in the fifth inning, but I over-managed, and we came away empty-handed when Lombardi was thrown out on the back end of an attempted double-steal.

Voiselle was going steady. Milton struck out the side. It was 0-0 at the end of six.

Hausman was thrown out stealing in the top of the seventh, killing a small rally.

"Hang in there, boys," I muttered under my breath.

I was glad to see the poor part of the Friends' batting order in the bottom of the seventh. Sister Melissa led off. Danny rolled the yellow and the white dice. Easy out. One gone. Milton, the pitcher, stepped in. (I almost gave him a round of applause; he was pitching a four-hitter.) Yellow and white rolled again. I looked at the dice, stunned. Milton clobbered one. I examined the yellow die and the scoring card again. It was 1-0, Friends over Giants.

No scoring in the eighth. We opened the ninth inning with a couple of breaks—they made two errors. (The young kids were feeling the pressure.) A force out, a pop out and a walk followed. The bases were loaded, two out and Voiselle, my weak-hitting pitcher coming up.

I checked the rules. "A good hitter may be inserted as a pinch-hitter for a fair hitter or a weak hitter during the game."

I made my move. I put down the yellow die (sending Voiselle back to the bench) and the pinch-hitter into the scorebook. (Ace Adams was warming up in the bull-pen.) I placed the blue die into the hand already holding the accompanying white one. ("O.K., Milton," I had whispered condescendingly.)

It didn't work out. Ducky Medwick lifted a lazy fly ball to Frankie in center field, and a bunch of third-graders had beaten my 1945 Giants, 1-0.

"Way to hang in there, Milton," screamed his excited seven-year-old manager.

I shot a dagger look at him.

"Tomorrow," I began threateningly, "tomorrow … you get Van Lingo Mungo."

Another confused look from Danny, with a trace of fear.

"That's my pitcher," I explained, with more than a trace of bitterness. "For tomorrow's game."

"Oh." A nod of relief. "I'm just stickin' with Milton."

6

Trying to Go Home Again

The Manchester Journal, April 25, 1974

Six years after our family moved from Long Island to Vermont, and more than a dozen years since I left the first school at which I taught, I decided it was time I went back to see what I had left. Who I had left. And, perhaps, figure out who I had taken with me. The return begged more questions than it answered. Can impressions be strong and confusing at the same time? It seemed that was the case.

The names of the few of the folks I speak about have been changed for reasons of discretion. I was not discreet when I first wrote the article, figuring the people named would not come across a newspaper published in a small Vermont town. And it was well before anything called internet access.

Valley Stream, New York—Many Manchesterites are Vermonters by adoption, and I am one of that number. Now I return for the first time in many years to the town and school which, seventeen years ago, opened a door and revealed a direction.

Valley Stream is just over the line from the Borough of Queens in New York City, and the fifty-year-old Wheeler Avenue School has its footing just in-bounds on the Nassau County side of that line.

My return to the halls of this school is motivated by a moderate curiosity hidden in the guise of a business suit. The pockets are filled with "remembrances of things past." But memory has a knack of inventing more than it remembers. Invention then becomes the mother of nostalgia, and it is far too easy to become distracted by the little tyke.

Thomas Wolfe's warning, "You Can't Go Home Again" meant little to me. We can go home again, I felt, if we're careful. I took the time en route to answer a few precautionary questions from a list we adopted Vermonters might keep handy for such occasions. The list (a mental one, you understand) included some pointed queries, such as:

What did we leave and why?
What did we take with us?
What part of ourselves did we leave behind?
What are we looking for when we return?
How do we recognize what we're looking for?

Well, you see, the *answers* will determine the nature and extent of our reactions; the questions themselves are not that useful. As I pass through the Wheeler Avenue School entrance my nostalgia anti-body count is probably not very high.

Nor does it get higher when I pass Room 114, my first classroom—and room 112, the room of Miss Wiklund (later to be Mrs. Dorfman). The kindling of reminiscence is aglow, but though small fires may warm us, big fires will burn us.

There are reminders of pleasant days, but many who took part in the events of those days are gone with the days. And most of those people who remain do not find daily routines in familiar surroundings conducive to dreaming.

We're told, predictably, that we haven't changed a bit. As if they know us now; as if they knew us then. But their smiles indicate the security we all feel when saying, "Nothing's changed." And we smile back, at the same time confirming and veiling the harmless deceit.

No surprises reveal themselves. In fact, a semi *déjà vu* is experienced in the recollection of a fragment of a poem by John Fowles.

> Old friends. One has them.
> They help one grow up,
> One knows them more and more;
> One knows them more and more
> And suddenly too much.
>
> It cannot be burked. One day,
> Too much. You see it, seeing
> Them here with you in your room:
> How they have at last become
> Reversed in the monstrous telescope,
> No longer old Friends, but milked
> Phenomena perfectly known,
> Indexed, mapped, immensely small.
>
> And then, like Hadrian, you build the wall.

Here is Claude, who has found what he always wanted and now pretends to have forgotten the sadder days of uncertain searching. And Lester, who has given up the search and pretends his days are not sad. And Blaine, who found only a mirage and ignores each new day's prospects. Greater griefs are mute.

Of course, much is here which is good, but sugared words for the past are too often used to coat a bitter present. (We sing, "Those were the days, my friend" with a gusto that is disconcerting.) The hours pass; business is taken care of; a genuine hand is clasped in parting. The exit is made surreptitiously.

Thomas Wolfe again, speaking autobiographically through Eugene Gant in *Look Homeward, Angel*, asks his beloved dead brother, "Where is the world?"

"No where," Ben said. "You are the world."

And so we all may be. At least, it might help us to think so. Particularly when going home again, because ultimately we may see that we no longer belong there, and that we probably haven't really gone 'home' after all.

7

Dear Visitor: Enjoy Our Home

The Vermont Times, September, 1974

Anita and I decided to travel to the birthplace of her parents, the Åland Islands, thousands of skerries scattered in the Baltic Sea between Sweden and Finland. School was out for the summer and the kids were also looking forward to the prospect—and meeting some of the one hundred (no kidding) first cousins with whom Anita would reacquaint herself. She had been there last as a teenager. It would be my first visit.

We had good friends living on Long Island (they're still in the same house they were then), and they were mildly interested in the idea of staying in our Vermont home for a few days, while we were gone.

At the same time, I was contacted by the editor of a state newspaper—published once a month. The gentleman had seen some of my writings in The Manchester Journal *and was interested in having me write something for his* Vermont Times.

Though thinking about having people stay in our house while we were away—something I wasn't all that pleased with, as close as I might be to the visitors—I was also thinking of a topic for the piece the editor wanted. I came up with the idea of a letter, a format I would use quite often in the future.

This was the first of its kind for me. The letter's premise was that folks had asked to stay in our house while we were gone. No one had asked. So, though I addressed it to our Long Island friend, it was not really meant for him—or his wife. Maybe they would have asked, had they not read 'the letter.'

As a device, it was well received—by my editor, at least. He boldly advertised my presence on the first page.

"The Dorfman Letter: Welcome to Vermont. Manchester wit Harvey Dorfman knows how to make a guest welcome. The first of a series of humorous comments from Mr. Dorfman."

He was hopeful.

Dear Gerard:

Certainly you are welcome to use our home while we are away. What good fortune for us both that your vacation coincides with our trip abroad. As you noted so perceptively in your last communication, there are indeed a few details you might be advised of beforehand.

First, I thought it would be proper to have you garage your car at night. (We don't really wish to have people see vehicles with out-of-state plates parked in our driveway. Bad for the neighborhood, you know.) Don't be alarmed when you open the garage door; the pile of bottles and cans within is not refuse. Since this blockade must be removed, would you at the same time box or bag these returnables (your state ought to consider this ecologically sound practice) and bring them to the local supermarket? (Please be so careful not to break any bottles while coming down the mountain on the washboard road.)

As I computed yesterday, there should be $56.70 coming to you in deposit money. I'll leave what we empty between now and our departure on the kitchen table, and you can add what they bring in to my figure. I'd just as soon split it with you seeing as, for five loads at ten cents a mile (plus wear and tear) to and from town, you should get something out of your chore. (I just worked it out, and you're doin' right decent, as my neighbor would say.)

And yes, it is lovely sitting out back in the shadow of the mountain at this time of year, and if you mow the lawn I'm sure you'll receive your share of the seasonal glory, be it sunlight or shade.

Of course, our pets do need care, as you seem to understand. But only of a perfunctory nature, for the most part. The fish are no trouble, but you'd probably be wise to change the water in the bowl because, with the chill of the night air, you'll want to keep the windows shut. A fresh bowl makes for more pleasant sleeping. (If you have allergies or polyps, then don't bother. It will be of no consequence to the fish.)

The cats are fed twice a day; the food is in the closet above the can opener. One note on that: you'll notice some cans of Alpo dog food in the closet, along with the cat food cans. Well, I did real well on a half gross of the Alpo at auction. But the cats have been watching the finicky-Morris ad on TV, so you have to mix one-third cat food with two-thirds dog food. Put it into the Osterizer and turn to 'grind.' (If you do not quite get the hang of making the blend—and you'll be able to tell by the cats' behavior—adjust the recipe according to whether they're acting more doggy than catty, etc.)

The rabbit gets pellets once a day, some greens at another feeding and water as needed. He likes his exercise, being alone as he is, and you'll see a leash hanging from the pencil sharpener above the garbage pails in the garage. If you're not entirely satisfied with conditions under and around his hutch, there's a bag of lime and a shovel adjacent to the work bench.

The wood pile, by the way, is low, and if you wish to bring some birch logs home with you (as mentioned in your letter) to decorate your artificial fireplace, you'd better get the chainsaw operating. (Bad plug, I believe; no real problem.) The gas can is empty, but you'll need some petrol for the mower anyhow, so save yourself a trip down off the mountain and cram the gas container in with your lightest load of soda bottles and beer cans.

I know you used to enjoy a shower on occasion, but I forgot whether or not you preferred a fine spray. (Fortunately, you are handy, in the event you do.) Some holes in the nozzle seem to be blocked up and the water sort of pounds on you. It's a good workout actually, but I don't recommend it for the wife or children. (Sorry about the bath tub, but I had a bit of an upset and went after an army of invading ants with the wrong spray can. Anita refused to clean it up, and it's on there for posterity I would guess. But give it a try; you always liked a challenge.)

Also, the refrigerator repairman promised he'd be by as soon as his unemployment check arrived in the mail. (Gas prices up here have taken a toll on every mode of life, believe me.)

Finally, don't concern yourself with taking the garbage to the dump; we have a nice fellow who makes a regular collection every Tuesday pre-dawn. (The timing of your arrival will be perfect.) Just be certain to put out the trash cans on Monday night. If you happen to hear a metallic cacophony during the mid-night hours, it is probably our neighbor's dog rummaging. He'll make a mess if you allow him, but what you'll find very effective is to run out and sprint at him for thirty yards or so, clapping your hands together quite vigorously over your head. That will serve a dual purpose, as it discourages most of the bears that often loiter in the area.

Otherwise—you are on your own. Again, let me welcome you to our home and to our state, and if you really enjoy yourself, feel free to stay an extra day.

Cordially,

H.A.

P.S. Don't forget to sign a guest book. (We surely would appreciate the kindness of your picking up one for us at a local shop. You'll be our FIRST, and we wouldn't have it any other way!)

8

The Udder Side of the Mountain

The Vermont Times, October, 1974

This 'udder' Dorfman letter is included because its topic was a contentious one in and about town at the time. A State's Attorney in Maine had taken it to a national level.

Vermont was holding out against the wave of state lotteries cascading into New England. (Our state had also resisted roadside billboard advertising and McDonald's restaurants.) Vermont was the only New England state without a lottery.

The letter was addressed to an invented relative, one who had changed his residency—and, as a result, his state of mind.

Dear Elmont:

Yes, cousin, I have been reading about the lottery problem which your U.S. Attorney has brought into the national headlines. I can't say I'm surprised.

I guess I've been berating you for six years now, ever since you moved to Maine. But time has proved me right again, I'm sorry (and a little proud) to say. After all, no good can come from living in a state that's wanting for grass. No grass means no cows, and people just don't seem to act quite right in places where there aren't enough cows around.

It was only a matter of time before your people hooked up with the lottery. And now, just as the first pass of the dice has been made (so to speak), your man Mr. Mills, has hollered, "Craps!" (so to speak). As you say, cousin, he has "stirred up more fuss than a llama gettin' a crew cut." (I'm willing to risk an Eisenhower dollar that it destroyed Miss Maine's chances of even receiving the Miss Congeniality Award at the Miss America Pageant.)

You ask what I think about the situation. Well, it's difficult to think about other people's problems. I don't mean to be cold and indifferent, Elmont, but you know perfectly well that Vermont is now the only New England state without a lottery. So it's only too tempting to cast the first stone, since, over here, we're free from sin (so to speak). But since you did ask ...

First of all, you're not going to get me going on the legality issue. All those legal 'experts' in Washington can spend their time with that one. (Anyhow, what's lawful is, more often than not, what's compatible with the ideas of the 'expert' who has jurisdiction or power. That reminds me of my neighbor's view of lawyers. He says they're built like dice; they lie on one side, but most often on the wrong one.)

Well, I don't want to put your nose in it, Elmont, but it all goes back to cows and right thinking. "Gamblin's a revolt against boredom," you tell me. But sensible people bear well what they're accustomed to. As a former Vermonter, you ought to understand that.

Here's something for you to think about. Remember Mahatma Gandhi? He said some very wise things. One idea he had was that gambling was worse than the plague or the quake. "It destroys the soul within," he said. I'd like to remind you that the man lived in a country that, to this day, worships and venerates the cow. "Cow protection is our gift to the world," Gandhi used to say. Are you getting my message, cousin?

As a former baseball fan and a diehard Yankee rooter, you've surely heard of Phil Rizzuto. He announces your team's game on radio and television these days. Do you know what his favorite saying is?—"Holy cow!" Imagine that. He's been shouting it for years.

Now a child growing up in a home where a father mouths a cliché of that sort is bound to be influenced. Mind control; subliminal learning. Call it what you will; it sank in. And that child grew to find where it was at (so to speak). Penny Rizzuto picked up and moved herself to Vermont a few years ago. She lives right here in Manchester.

Have I made any sense to you? I just wish cows could talk. They'd tell you, Elmont. I'm certain they hold a valuable secret, and it isn't the winning number in your next month's lottery.

For now, I'll close with a passage from Gooke's Meditations which strikes me as particularly appropriate.

It is sayd there be a raunge of mountaynes in the Easte,
on one side of which certain conducts are imorall, yet on the
other side they are holden in good esteeme; whereby the
mountaineer is much conveenyenced, for it is given to him
to goe downe eyther way and act as it shall suite his moode...

You're on the wrong side of the mountain, Elmont. The udder side (so to speak) is the side for you. Come back home, even if it has to be after the 90-day injunction.

Fondly,

H.A.

P.S. Anita is pestering me to tell you that she just missed the trifecta at Green Mountain Race Track the other night.

9

The Umpire Is Always Right,
Except When He Is Proved Wrong

The New York Times, October 20, 1974

Ecclesiastes had it right. There really isn't much new under the sun. Same old, same old. Baseball umpires are still under the bright lights of public scrutiny and, if many of their recent calls can be any indication, that glare still gets in their eyes. Fans and those closer to the game have been upset enough to provoke some action: taped replays of questionable calls. Many of the calls, not all. Have trust and respect for these arbiters been lost? Well, the greatest accolade coming to an umpire (aside from Doug Harvey's induction into the Hall of Fame in 2010), was praise for Jim Joyce. The praise was for his confession, not his call. A very bad call, one that cost a Detroit pitcher the formal recognition of having thrown a 'perfect game.'

But as for the scrutiny, the criticism, the indignation, the search for solutions: same old, same old. Which led me to this piece, written 37 years ago. Since then, having been in major league dugouts for fourteen years, I find my respect for major league umpires has diminished. I've witnessed too many power plays, much mean-spirited behavior and/or defensive behavior, short fuses—and spitefulness. This is not the place to provide specific examples. Sorry. The reader will just have to take my word on faith.

All the supportive *words written below at an earlier time should indicate my desire to be supportive—on merit.*

Joe Klein is the manager of a farm team in the Texas Rangers organization. A few weeks ago he asked, rhetorically as well as philosophically: "In this whole world ... in this whole world, can't forty-eight guys be found who can be super umpires?"

Recently, the Major League Baseball Players' Association provided an answer of sorts: Not yet. The results of a player poll taken in the National and American Leagues intended for players and league offices only, became public information. Only three umpires received anything resembling "super" grades. Forty-five to go, Joe Klein.

Ten other umpires were adjudged to be "above average," 18 "average," 13 "below average" and 4 "poor." It seems appropriate to examine the legitimacy and the possible utility of this precedent-setting public disclosure.

Videotaped replays, shown to large television audiences, have begun to heat umpires' blue collars to a degree anticipated by neither Gabriel Fahrenheit nor Leo Durocher. Recent flagrant boo-boos, replayed and discussed during nationally televised baseball games, have left unfavorable and indelible impressions in the collective mind's eye of the viewing fans.

Barbed commentary by broadcasters, notably Joe Garagiola and Phil Rizzuto, has added color to the umpires' already reddened necks. Retorts through the media by these same men in blue seemed transparently defensive. A blown call is a blown call is a blown call.

What has already begun to happen to the umpires' image requires diagnosis and prescription—by league officials and, even more so, by the umpires themselves. Let them be reminded by Francis Bacon (or was it Bill Veeck?) that those who will not apply new remedies must expect new evils. Ironically, the public disclosure of the results of the poll might well be an initial remedy, rather than the fatal poison many umpires consider it to be.

The old graven image of the omniscient-indifferent-God-figure-baseball-umpire never really fooled anyone. A baseball devotee understands a poor call when he thinks he sees one, and viewing it in slow motion from six angles reinforces the fan's judgment. In other words, the fan now knows what he always used to suspect, sitting back there in Row W of the grandstand: umpires kick one occasionally, some more occasionally than others. Players and managers have always known it. So have the umps, Bill Klem notwithstanding. But I would hope that an infrequent misjudgment is not sinful.

Neither is it a sin for the fan-in-the-street to know which umpires the players consider to be best (least sinful, if you insist) and worst. After all, the legitimate aim of criticism is to direct attention to excellence. The players' ratings of umpires were accompanied by brief comments "intended to be constructive." These notations appear to be valuable prescriptions for the cure of tarnished reputations.

Significantly, the more important qualities of a healthy umpire, according to the players, are attentiveness, effort and reaction. Judgment may be implied in a number of other terms (e.g. "consistency"), but attitude (i.e. hustle, control) impresses the players more.

It's a fact that managers and general managers rate umpires every year. Fortunately for all concerned, these ratings remain confidential, since simple mathematics precludes a manager's objectivity when measuring the caliber of an umpire.

If the manager loses a pennant or a higher position in the league standing by a game or few, and if he recalls an umpire's call or ruling "costing me that game" (that's the way managers talk, you know), then he can just as readily blame umpires for costing him his job when he loses it. The ratio of single games to a team's season schedule is less than propitious, if one is to faithfully accept a manager's umpire-rating-sheet as gospel, even if you held Diogenes' lamp over a shoulder while he filled it out. May Danny Ozark forgive me.

On the other hand, a player's statistics speak for themselves at contract time. They are public knowledge, and it is difficult to convince the boss that in 500 times at bat a hitter's average has been dramatically affected by poor ball-strike calls. Similar analogies may be applied to pitchers, to out-safe calls and to concession sales. The umpire cannot take the rap for everyone's poor performance. A player can be both objective and comfortable at the same time.

And who else but the player sees the umpires going about their business on a regular basis? The third base coaches? The trainers? The owners? The batboys?

What it simmers down to is simply this: Someone who performs in public cannot escape judgment of some sort by all who view the performance. So let the players' voices be heard. Let the fans discover what it actually takes to be a superior. Let those fans discover who the fine ones are. Let the umpires on their winter rubber-chicken circuit enlighten their audiences by providing more insights into the demands of umpiring and fewer jokes that demean the profession.

Let the players continually refine their instrument of evaluation, and let them sophisticate their attitude toward it. Let major league officials reappraise their system of umpire promotion and retention. And let the umpires open their eyes to what may be valid criticism and applicable advice.

Then, and only then, might fans cease to malign an essential and highly respectable functionary. Then might fans appreciate the subtleties in the work done by these dedicated and responsible men. Then might the players' ratings exclude such an ambiguous rating as "average." Then might the New York Mets choose to participate in the poll. Then might umpiring excellence prevail. And then, perhaps, will the board of directors of the Major League Umpires Association chose not to ignore and disparage the players' ratings.

Until then, hang tough, Joe Klein.

10

A Tongueless Grief

The Manchester Journal, December 19, 1974

We never know what demons swirl around in the psyches of those with whom we come in contact regularly.

David Monty, the librarian at Manchester's Mark Skinner Library was an introverted, overweight bachelor who tended to be reclusive. He was also brilliant, had an acerbic wit—and was responsive to those who took the time to engage him beyond his surrounding Dewey's decimals.

I was one of the few who did that. (The only one?) We engaged in verbal jousts—when we saw each other (almost always in the library) and in print. He would write witty and challenging letters to the editor after reading one of my columns, and I would respond in kind. People in town thought we had an antagonistic relationship—that we didn't like each other. David, particularly, enjoyed the ruse.

He had expanded his vista—helping to serve dinner at the local school, a fund-raising spaghetti meal I had organized. He seemed so happy to be part of the activity.

Weeks later, he went downstairs to the conference room of the library and took his life.

There will be many interpretations. Some will call it bravery; some will call it cowardice. Others a confession, self-criticism, lost hope. They are all definitions, and they do not matter. They are words, and words are only shadows of deeds. David Monty's final deed was one which cast its own shadow. Still, we struggle to gain some light as we talk ourselves deeper into the darkness. Yet we must talk.

I did not know David very well, and, for that matter, I wonder how many people in town felt they did. *Really* know him. Because that is the only way to make such a claim. How many people *do* we know, in that case? And how, then, can every life be an example, as the sages say?

David and I enjoyed sharing books and laughter with each other. The repartee at the Mark Skinner Library and lately at Community Reading Council meetings was lively and good-natured. He had a special appreciation for our "exchange" in the pages of *The Journal* last spring—and for the queries we each received (and reported to each other) relating to "obvious" lack of amity between us. (More laughter.) But this is beginning to sound eulogistic, which is saying too much too late.

Those who witnessed his dedicated and cheerful efforts before and during the Right-to-Read Supper last week, those who saw his smiling countenance on the front page of *The Guide* last week, those who might have seen more of the same elsewhere apparently saw only as much as they were allowed to see—a façade, at that. The sorrow behind it was secret and undoubtedly very deep. We will be tempted to come forward with clues. (Retrospect makes geniuses of us all.) What will they tell us next?

The message, so far as I can fathom, is not to be found in our mouths or in a non-existent final note. Can it simply be that we are too preoccupied with licking our own small wounds to notice the larger wounds of others—some of them inflicted by us? That we are too often too frozen to dissolve our selfishness? That we are always too late with each other?

David Monty was a classicist. He had a taste for philosophy. But unlike Cicero, he could not use it as an ultimate antidote for sorrow. I know neither the nature of his grief nor its duration. Its depth has been measured. Best grief is tongueless Emily Dickinson wrote, "and a rack couldn't coax a syllable—now."

But can we somehow coax the right syllables from within ourselves? Time answers such questions. Do we think we have the right not to make the attempt? David Monty has provided that answer.

11

The Chocolate Surprise Incident

The Manchester Journal, January 9, 1975

It's reassuring to know that twenty-plus years prior to 'the incident' described and thirty-five years since, the upper echelons of the military had and continues to demand strict standards of behavior—from the lower echelons.

As a former Naval Reservist (ten years with an Honorable Discharge—no active duty, plenty of Tuesday nights devoted to thoughtless and/or inconsequential activities—often just foolish), I had the opportunity to observe and participate in situations which could compete with the one addressed in this article. Can this incident really be an authentic representation? Yes. I can vouch for that.

I'll let "The Chocolate Surprise Incident" speak for itself. (Were Mark Twain to speak for it, he'd remind us that man is the only animal that blushes—or has cause to. Especially man dressed in a uniform signifying high rank.)

It is probably too early to assign the case its proper place in military-law history. The least we can say at this time is that laws are not always silent in the midst of arms, and, predictably, neither are lawyers. At the risk of being frivolous, I'd call it a classic. Be your own judge. Be your own jury, for that matter. Cuddle up in a cold metal folding chair and—now hear this. (That's Navy lingo.)

THE BACKGROUND—Leon L. Louie, a 19-year-old Seabee, was recently court-martialed by the Navy for throwing a chocolate pie in a warrant officer's face. Mr. Louie was brought up on charges of assault because he tossed the pie in Chief Warrant Officer Timothy P. Curtin's face at the morning muster of their 700-man battalion.

The civilian attorney retained by Mr. Louie, a fellow who calls himself William Smith (and who can blame him?), told the press that his client had been part of some Seabees' planned practical joke to raise morale (and who can blame them?). He vowed to go all out in defense of his client. The legal fees were partly paid in advance by a group of Asian law students. (Mr. Louie is Chinese-American.)

THE TRIAL—The prosecution opened by reading Chapters Two and Three from *The Bluejackets' Manual* ('BJM'), 14th edition, entitled respectively, "Naval Customs and Courtesy" and "Naval Discipline."

From the context below the heading, "Other Serious Offenses," the prosecution quoted the following: "Fighting and disturbance—To strike another person in the Navy is an offense punishable by court-martial. No matter what differences a Navy man may have with another member of the Service, he must remember that the respect due the Service is more important than the argument at hand. To forget this rule will involve the man in serious difficulties. In case there is just cause for argument or disagreement, the matter should be taken up with the company commander or division officer."

The lawyer pointed his pinkie (an effective technique, judging by the reaction of those present in the room) at Mr. Louie and warned him that conviction for this offense could mean imprisonment for six months, forfeit of his pay and a dishonorable discharge from the Navy.

Prosecution then felt compelled, since tears were welling up in his eyes, to read from Chapter 16 (same text), "Your Career in the Navy." Under the heading, "Some of the Opportunities," the prosecution read item #8 with obvious emotion: "A permanent job. *No fears of depression* (emphasis through choking sounds) or *Loss of work* (more of the same emphasis)." The point being ...?

Prosecution ended this first presentation by gasping from the same chapter the heading, "What the Navy Expects from You." The rest of his words were inaudible. He slumped into his chair.

The Defense rose smartly and read from the very section prosecution had almost silently cited. Said the Defense (in a voice remarkably like Dennis Morgan's in the movie *Desert Song*)—"Fighting Spirit. A good Navy man stays with a hard job. He never says, 'I can't.'"

Defense then went on to explain how Mr. Louie was chosen as the designated thrower (restrained giggle from Prosecution, an apparent baseball devotee and probable all-around good sport) by the other enlistees. The Defense continued, "They had just returned from duty in the wilds of Puerto Rico, and everyone's morale was low. It (the pie throwing) seems to have been a battalion joke and my client was nominated to do the job. Everyone laughed (when it reached its target), including Chief Warrant Officer Curtin, and no one can believe that the Navy is so uptight (civilian lingo) about morale that they would throw a special court-martial against the kid."

Everyone in the room looked puzzled, since the thought was that lawyer Smith would question the Navy's uptightness about discipline, not morale. (A tool room trick perhaps.) Defense further questioned why the court-martial procedure should be followed. "Usually minor infractions are handled by a captain's mast or possibly a summary court-martial," said Mr. Smith. "I've researched naval legal history, and I haven't found a single case of a court-martial for pie-throwing."

Prosecution then discussed "hostility" between officers and enlisted men because of a variety of discipline problems.

Defense stated that this very fact was what made enlistees play their joke, for the sake of better morale. He said the whole case smacked of racism; a white sailor wouldn't have been court-martialed for a practical joke.

Prosecution supposed, with a wry grin and that pinkie finger again (and we still can't blame him) that the use of vanilla custard pie would have precluded court-martial.

Defense was glad to hear that both sides finally agreed about something.

Recess was declared.

THE WITNESS—Defense, with a dazzling touch of civilian genius, produced as a witness comedian Soupy Sales, who said he was an "expert" on the entertainment value of pie-throwing. Mr. Sales said with a broad smile that he had received "more than 19,000 (pies in the face) since 1950. It's always a very funny incident. It's the thing you can really do to relieve tension without hurting anyone."

Prosecution was slow to rise from his chair—apparently to object.

Defense preemptively sprang from his seat and reminded the court that even Chief Warrant Officer had laughed when hit with Mr. Louie's pie.

Mr. Sales' eyes glowed; Officer Curtin's lowered; Defense crowed; Prosecution glowered.

Prosecution reached under his chair and extracted a pie from a paper bag. He walked deliberately toward the Defense …

THE RECIPE—Chocolate Surprise Custard Pie—Bake at 425 for 10 minutes, then at 350 for 35 to 40 minutes. (Makes an 8-inch pie)

Sift together—1 cup sifted all-purpose flour (Omit ale if using self-rising flour); 1 teaspoon sugar and ¼ teaspoon salt into mixing bowl.

Cut in—1/3 cup shortening until the size of small peas.

Combine—3 tablespoons water and 1 tablespoon vinegar. Sprinkle over flour mixture, stirring with a fork until dough is moist enough to hold together. Form into a ball.

Roll out—on floured surface to a circle 1 ½ inches larger than inverted 8-inch pie pan. Fit loosely into pan. Fold edge to form standing rim; flute. Chill while making chocolate custard filling.

For Chocolate Custard Filling—Combine 1 egg, 3 yolks, ½ cup sugar and 1 teaspoon vanilla in mixing bowl. Beat with fork to combine.

Add—2 ounces grated or shaved semi-sweet chocolate. DO NOT STIR. Carefully pour into pie shell.

Bake as directed above.

NOTE—Mess with meringue topping at your own risk; you can get the firing squad for throwing one of those.

12

The Pinewood Project

The Manchester Journal, February 6, 1975

In our family, my reputation as an un-handyman reached epic proportion a long time ago. Over the years, the word spread beyond the limits of our walls—floors and ceiling. As I draw nearer to my dotage, the little skill I have (I'm cutting myself some slack here) is less in evidence—if ever in evidence in the first place. But family members can be tolerant. Love does that.

My son, Dan, on the other dexterous hand, has been a skilled Mr. Fix-it since he was a young boy. He's even created things through use of impressive skills and sophisticated tools. He has made beautiful writing pens, sought after by a local tourist shop. He's built horse stables and barns single-handedly. But this piece is about my liabilities, rather than his assets. Let me say that I'm grateful that he lives 15 miles from where Anita and I reside in North Carolina. He is only a call away when urgent attention must be paid to—say—a broken toilet paper holder.

Fathers get some pride in their children's achievements, and I am not an exception. After all is said (by me) and done (by him), I do believe I served as an example for him. One he did not wish to emulate.

This piece suggests, to a small extent, my skill level, his understanding tolerance and the shared feeling we have for each other.

It was a call to duty—as simple as that. The warm-hearted will stoke their inner fires and call it devotion; the cynical will call it competitiveness; the flippant will call it fun. It was a call to duty—and that call was loud enough.

A while ago my eight-year-old son came home from a Cub Scout meeting with a fistful of pine and a head full of notions. Enthusiastically, he introduced me to the "Pinewood Derby Plan" and its accompanying kit. The Derby, I am now able to inform those of you who need the information, is an annual Cub Scout father-and-son project. A block of wood was provided in the kit, to be shaped into a race car, prepared and decorated for Derby Night and raced at that time against all Cub comers. "That time" was last Thursday night.

I'll try to offer an objective, though personal, account of one team's involvement. But first, some necessary background notes.

1. The father's father, an apartment dweller all his life, had an aversion for tools and their related function.
2. As a result, the father thought the tool 'screwdriver' was named after the drink—having become familiar with the latter first.
3. Though thanks to the Meredith Press *Handyman's Book* the father has made remarkable progress, his wife and children are not able to speak of his manual dexterity with any sincere trace of familial pride. Their assessment is honest and accurate and is accepted as it is offered—with a mixture of good-natured understanding and no hope for the future. (Some fine family jokes still endure, all dealing with past handyman projects.)

The aforenoted background seems adequate as an introduction to an *a priori* presentation. The chronology of events leading up to Derby night follows:

- Using primitive tools—a hammer and chisel (chisel borrowed from a neighbor), a shape for the car is effected. (Three hours and some casual profanity from the father.)
- Father and son show wife/mother and daughter/sister the roughed out model.
- Wife/mother says it looks like a hearse; daughter asks if it's a soap carving.
- Father and son go back to garage workbench, to hammer, chisel. A bit more sincere profanity.
- Team re-reads specification sheet and building hints, underlining key passages.
- Team then quits for the day.
- Team resumes activity: filing, sanding, inserting axles, splitting one, reciting double-entendre limerick (father's creation), repairing broken axle, mistakenly shortening it, etc. (Elmer's glue, we love you.)
- Son praises father's craftsmanship with assurances that product is top-quality.
- Father points out flagrant defects, e.g. crooked wheels, etc.
- Son philosophizes on value of project done jointly.
- Father smiles and enjoys feeling of pride (in son, not car).
- Father files plastic nubs of wheels, too forcefully.
- Father says wheels look like the ones on Fred Flintstone's car.
- Both laugh, quit work.
- Son comes home from school, tells father about friend's car, "a beauty, like it came from Macy's."
- Father picks up unfinished team car. "Vroom, vroom."
- Both laugh.

- Paint job is started. Step one: orange spray.
- Next day, step two: blue trim. Father: "Looks like a Nassau County garbage truck. Son laughs. (He's never seen a Nassau County garbage truck.) Both slap a knee, quit work.
- Son comes home from school with plastic driver given by friend/owner of Macy-looking car.
- Too much eleventh-hour trouble to cut out a place for driver's legs. Team chops them off, glues driver into seat.
- Derby eve arrives. Final touches made: put on numbers, oil wheels, cover slipping wheel pins with more plastic wood.
- Father mock-announces big night's race at dinner table. Various catastrophes involving car # 80 offered with an assortment of renditions.
- Total man/boy hours spent on project figured (not for public consumption) on calculator before departure to race site, the high school gym.

The Pinewood Derby itself was a fine show. Many of the cars were indeed spectacular in appearance and/or performance. Car # 80, predictably, had some trying moments. To begin with the shortened front axle prevented the car from properly fitting over the track's lane strip. A pit stop was required before the warm-up runs even began! I tugged at the wheels in an attempt to widen the base and wished that this would be a Demolition Derby instead. The plastic driver was dislodged permanently in the process.

Meanwhile, a trio of Cub fathers beside me provided disrespectful, hilariously appropriate commentary which kept the situation in proper focus for me. My concern was for my son however. He deserved a run for our efforts, at least. The wheels in my damp hands gave somewhat, but so did the axle angle. The official starter, after having waited patiently, placed the car on the track with thoughtful care. Two trials heats were to be run; the car remained relatively intact, though setting no track record, surely.

Shortly after the gate was released for the start of the real race, # 80 came to a grinding halt. It had gotten less than half-way down the slope. A dinner-table catastrophe had actualized. The car was taken from the track by its too-casual owner. The manner belied a normal degree of embarrassment to one witness. An adult friend—a track-side factotum—looked at the car and made an extemporaneous adjustment of the axle between heats.

Car # 80 had another opportunity, this time against the other fourth place finishers in previous heats. The orange and blue bomber came in second. A two-fingered signal was secretly flashed to me by the owner from the finish line across the gym, a facial display of pride further manifesting itself as he saw my nodding recognition.

Needless to say, car # 80 won no awards.

As we motored home in the darkness, we reviewed Pinewood Derby Week and our common collective faith (not in # 80, you understand). Good feelings provoked my companion to mouth a competition post-mortem typically heard at 19th holes and in the locker rooms of losers.

"If the wheels didn't get stuck, our car would have done great."

He was reminded that *IF* frogs had wings they wouldn't bump their butts on the ground.

It cut short conjecture-after-the-fact. The verities of life reasserted themselves. He leaned against my arm; I pulled at his hair and, beaming in the night, we followed our path home.

Postscript—The following year we produced a car that was not any more effective on the race track. But it did win an award. It was voted "The Kookiest Car"—a first-time category.

13

Lincoln Lore

The Manchester Journal, February 13, 1975

Two names of public/historical figures were referred to often within the walls of the apartment where I lived as a boy. Most of the references were for my enlightenment, since my sisters were considerably older, better educated and not in attendance all that often. (Mostly bedridden during my first twelve years, I was there for my father's instruction—always.)

The two names were Clarence Darrow and Abraham Lincoln. I was motivated to write a bit about Old Abe since his birthday was coming around—and I had no other topic in mind to write about. My father would have extolled Lincoln's wisdom; I was more impressed—in my youth—with Lincoln's wit. I remember a few stories here that introduced that appreciation.

Wednesday marked the one hundred sixty-sixth anniversary of Abraham Lincoln's birth. People still remember the day, of course, but schools remain open and the special nature of the celebration has diminished considerably.

Not the man, so far as I am concerned. Small wonder. As a lad I had *Bomba, the Jungle Boy* literally torn from my clutches and replaced by Sandburg's *The Prairie Years*. I fought parental intrusion and coercion, but the co-efficiency of the patriarch and Lincoln forced me to succumb. Honest Abe was captivating. Exit Bomba on his ephemeral elephant.

My father focused his great respect on Lincoln's "far-reaching cerebral powers." Many people had (and still have) a delectation for his compelling personality, his droll sense of humor. That's what hooked me. That and the fact that he retained it—refined it, perhaps—through the most difficult of times. Few public men (in high places particularly) manifest such a genuine and spontaneous warmth and wit. (Lincoln did *not* have a speech writer, you recall.) Stories illustrating this keen wit (and wisdom) are legion.

The first one I remember hearing (a favorite for a number of reasons and a generally well-known anecdote) told of an insecure and envious general in the army. Union generals in the War Between the States had been weak and ineffectual before the appointment of Ulysses S. Grant. The first Grant successes accented further his colleagues' failures. Lincoln was somewhat mollified, having finally acquired an authentic leader.

The story has it that one of the inept generals, acting as a representative of the others, went to the President to inform him of Grant's excessive drinking. One can envision Lincoln's thoughtful stance—the pause for effect—then: "Do get me the name of the whiskey he drinks; I would like to purchase a case of it for each of my other generals." The point and the condonation were clear. The complainant made a hasty departure.

Much was made of the man's "ugliness." An obnoxious dowager, after having stared at the President for an inordinate period of time, curtly advised him of her conclusion. "My, you're a homely man, Mr. Lincoln."

Lincoln leaned toward her and reviewed her countenance with his penetrating eyes. "The Lord must love homely persons, madam; he seems to have made so many of us."

So the story goes.

One incident had a forbidding fellow thrusting a pistol in Abe's face. The weapon-wielder explained that he had sworn an oath years before to shoot on the spot any man he might find who was uglier than he.

"Shoot me, then," said Abe, "for if I'm uglier than you I don't wish to live."

Lincoln enjoyed reading the many stories about him, both the mythical and the factual. His supposed favorite was recorded by B.A. Botkin, the noted folklorist.

"Two Quakeresses were traveling on the railroad and were heard discussing the probable termination of the war. 'I think,' said the first, 'that Jefferson (Davis) will succeed.'

'Why does thee think so?' asked the other.

'Because Jefferson is a praying man.'

'And so is Abraham a praying man,' objected the second.

'Yes, but the Lord will think Abraham is joking,' the first replied conclusively.

Doubtful. The Lord knows better.

Lord also knows we could use Abraham down here right now.

14

Relationship of Sports, Society, '75

The Rutland Herald, March 19, 1975

Living in Vermont was helpful to my 'career' as a journalist. The sports-writing part particularly. The Rutland Herald *had asked me to drive to Montreal (4 hours) and Boston (3 ½ hours) to cover some games and do features about the Expos and Red Sox. The geographical proximity of those teams to our state allowed for a fan base that the newspaper was well aware of.*

I thought those articles to be neither exceptional in their presentation nor special in content. (None is included in this book.)

The Managing Editor, however, was pleased with what was produced. He began to increase his requests for my work—and asked me to write a "commentary piece." I asked him what subject he wished me to comment on. He was taken aback by my question. A man with a quick and fertile mind, he said abruptly, "Er … how about a sports and society thing?" He asked if I had any idea what he was talking about. "Not at this moment," I said. He told me to give it some thought—and have the piece ready the next day.

So here it is. It seemed to me to be without much to commend itself—a pedestrian piece. But it's clear that the corruption of sport has accelerated, rather than decelerated, since this commentary was written. The cost of living has gone along for the ride (note the reference to cost of an academic year at Georgia Tech in 1975). Ticket prices for sporting events are outrageous; concessions prices are indigestible. Matters are also worse now thanks, in part, to youth league coaches and parents, technological advances, Madden football, So-and-So's basketball, hockey and snooker, TV poker—and the human condition, in general.

No hope in sight.

One needn't be a radical to question the merit of sport in our society these days—professional sports particularly. Yet, in a world which begs for answers to serious questions—questions of survival—sport still possesses a theoretical potential for playing a humanizing role. The bow, after all, can't always stand bent; human nature subsists, in part, because of relief of tension, and this relief often depends on some form of recreational outlet.

Unfortunately, within the roles of daily life, diminishingly small space can be found for expression of those physical characteristics which allow the common man to 're-create.' As a result, too many (do I dare say 'most?') of us take our sports second hand, as spectators.

The point is this: given the sociologists' view that the massification and consumption of American sport will be with us for some time to come, we must, as spectators, at least retain our own semblance of dignity and be able to recognize some of it in the game we watch, so as to feel that the consumership of sport is ennobling rather than degrading.

Guess what. I don't feel ennobled any longer, and I'm not happy about it. Of course I'm not alone. Just last week a veteran sportscaster-newsman in the Southwest announced that "enough is enough." He resigned, not because he hates sports, but because he hates what has happened to the sports he loves.

In part, Simeon Smith said: "Over the years I have watched the 'sports' world grow to the point where I can no longer regard it as sport. On all levels, professional, college, high school and, indeed, even on the grade school level, athletics in this country has become a business."

Smith touched upon the loss of "fun" (recreation!) in organized sport and chastised coaches at all school levels. He concluded his remarks by saying that he could no longer "approve of the manner in which our children are being raised when they become a part of the 'world of sports.' Amateur sports should be fun, and pro sports should be put in proper perspective."

Other samplings of commentary from last Sportsweek are *less* encouraging.

Item: Fred Shero, Philadelphia Flyers coach, on how to maintain team unity—"I'd do anything for my players. I'd lie, cheat and steal for them and they know it. That's why everyone works so well together on our team." (Watergate on ice.)

Item: Derek Sanderson of the New York Rangers, explaining why there are so many fights in hockey—"They fight because there's a lot of publicity in it and publicity brings money. The Flyers got a lot of publicity last season for fighting. Now the players get $1,000 an appearance at banquets." (Boston's Dave Forbes may need more than that for bail.)

Item: Daily photos of Catfish Hunter pitching, talking, walking, standing, sitting, counting and always smiling. (With P.T. Barnum smugness, and no wonder.)

Item: A televised tug-of-war between players from two baseball teams was billed as a battle to determine the 'super-team.' (Surely millions were at the end of their rope.)

Item: Roger Bisher, son of *Atlanta Journal* sports editor Furman Bisher, had been awarded a four-year athletic scholarship to Georgia Tech, worth about $10,000. *(How much THESE days?)* When this fact was brought to the fellow's attention, he was quoted as saying, "I'm just as selfish as the next SOB and if I don't get it (the scholarship), somebody else will." (Onward and upward, Rog—and Furm.)

There is more, needless to say. University of Jacksonville basketball players are being investigated in relation to shaving points last season. *(College players in NYC did this during my high school days—and were prosecuted.)* Their coach has resigned. Legalize betting, you say? Bill Walton (an enigma I leave for others to solve); the great debate on whether spiking the football is an ethnic gesture (it's illegal now for blacks and whites); Mark Spitz in Hollywood (ugh!); more, more, more.

More teams, more players, more dollars, more debasement. (Pity the poor contemporary bubble gum card collector. If frustration doesn't overcome him, bankruptcy will.) Less dignity, less quality, less fun, less ennoblement.

Professional athletics as we know it is sport that has become work. Like so much else, its proportion has gone far beyond our original intentions. At the same time, its purpose and ethic have both been distorted. Blame whomever you wish: the media, unions, agents, management, the players themselves. But if you don't like what's going on, move your own body around for a change. And keep your recreation dollar away from the sportsmonster.—Or blame yourself, the consumer.

15

The National Pastime or,
A Little Bit of Luck

The New York Times, April 6, 1975

Many people would be more respected for their opinions were it not for their uncontrollable need to express them.

An example to support my theory was the public pronouncement (I have no idea who initiated the suggestion) that betting on sporting events should be legalized, expanded and encouraged. (Today, ESPN would bang out a feature and call it "Inside the Lines." About betting lines, of course.)

Not that the concept of legalized gambling upset me. After all, my father was an amateur gambler (though a smart and effective one), and I sat at his feet and learned to share his enthusiasm for the activity, be it at a race track or in a bookie's parlor. But, as an adult, I could sense some downside to such a policy. I could also imagine some interesting possibilities. This piece tried to represent a few.

And, as usual, nothing ever came of all the excited gambling advocates' hopes.

'Let Us Now Praise Jimmy the Greek'
(A One-Act Clairvoyance)

Setting: The bleachers, Fenway Park, Boston. Opening game, 1975 season. Boston Red Sox vs. Milwaukee Brewers.

Characters: Father, a baseball devotee; Son, age 9; Vendors

The Commission on the Review of the National Policy Toward Gambling Chorale has completed the singing of "Luck Be a Lady Tonight."

Jimmy (the Greek) Snyder has just thrown out the first ball.

Father: Aren't you glad you came, boy? Beautiful weather, two small ones bet on Luis Tiant at 25-35 over Jim Slaton—and Dice Day, to boot.

Son: (Turning the management's gift over in his hands): Are they loaded, Dad?

Father (Laughing): In our favor, I hope.

Son: What's the bottom figure between you and the U.S. betting office?

Father: Ah, ha! 7 - 40 in our favor, boy. (Shouting) Play ball!

Son: Can I have some peanuts, Dad? There's a vendor.

Father: They don't sell peanuts at games anymore, son. Not enough money in it.

Son (pointing): Then what's that guy doing over there?

Father: Just listen, you'll hear. He's coming our way.

Vendor: Here you go! Three players for six hits. Pick 'em now! Last chance— game's startin.' Three players for six hits! At 5-to-1 odds! Last chance!

Father (Waving arm): Over here!

Vendor: Who's your pleasure, mister?

Father: Gimme Yaz, Rice and ...

Son (Shouting): Petrocelli!

Vendor looks at father for confirmation. Father shrugs
shoulders and hands a $10 bill to vendor, who records
the selection.

Vendor (Giving a receipt to father): The kid blew it for you, mister.

Father (Patting son's head, shrugging again, shouting): Play ball! Mow 'em down, Luis. Baby needs new shoes!

[ONE HOUR LATER]

Vendor: Pocket calculators here!

Father (Standing and applauding); *Bueno*, Luis, *bueno*. Keep mowing 'em down, *Amigo*. (Turning) How y'doin,' son?

Son (Playing with dice on seat): O.K., Dad. But I have to go to the men's room.

Father (Inattentively): Ho! The scorer must have Yaz in the six-hit pool, too. He gave him a hit on that play.

[MINUTES LATER]

Son: Dad.

Father: Ho, ho! Today's our day, boy. The ump has 10 big ones on the Sox, for sure!

Son (Shouting): Dad! (Lower) I have to go to the men's room.

Father: Oh, fine, son. Seven bits stake if you get there yourself.

Son (Resignedly): Sure, Dad.

[HOURS LATER]

The game has been completed; the son has not returned
from his sojourn. Father, after a brief post-game search,
discovers the boy cowering under the stands.

Father: Where ya been, son? Six to five you had a problem.

Son (With pained expression): No bet, Dad.

Father (Trying to raise the boy's spirits): You missed the three-straight hit parlay I nailed in the eighth—and Petrocelli got one of them! (Pause) Hey, what's wrong?

Son (Reluctantly): Well, I waited on line almost all of the time—and when it finally was my turn, I saw that those ... things ... (Makes a gesture)

Father: Urinals?

Son (Nods): ... Urinals were gone. There were slot machines instead.

Father: Holy Scarne! So that's why you were hiding out. Tough break, kid.

Son: Not all bad, Dad. I hit on three lemons.

Father: Aw right! And I hit a bingo on Little Luis Tiant, six hits and the parlay I was telling you about. C'mon, boy. Eight to ten we can find you a money belt to go along with some new pants.

Son (With confidence restored): Dad, are the Detroit Tigers named after Nathan Detroit?

Both exit whistling "Take Me Out to the Ball Game."

[CURTAIN]

16

Call This Phenom's Story
a Change of Pace

The Boston Globe, May 9, 1975

I debated with myself about the inclusion in the book of this feature article. But my prevailing thought was that the subject of the article, a young baseball player whose psyche, body and performance—his life, in other words, had been adversely affected by extenuating circumstances—was one of many guys (different names, different situations) I met over the years. He was a kind of precursor of my career change. What I learned from the young man, David Clyde, when doing this piece, I would often make use of during future interventions with professional athletes.

As I write these words, Steven Strasburg, another precocious and highly publicized young pitcher, is rehabilitating after having had Tommy John surgery to repair his pitching elbow.

David Clyde is fifty-five years old and has been watching—and commenting on— Strasburg's experience. What Clyde knows—and everyone else should know—is that Strasburg has been treated in an entirely different manner—conservatively and cautiously by the Washington Senators, his team. And he has an extensive support team (Strasburg is represented by the Scott Boras Corporation, the group I work for these days), whereas what little direction Clyde was given steered him 'off the cliff.'

Strasburg signed out of college, Clyde out of high school. By the time David Clyde was nineteen, he was divorced, alcoholic and injured.

I'd been writing a weekly baseball column for the Berkshire Sampler. *Each piece featured a player on the Pittsfield Rangers, a Texas Double-A farm team. (None of them included in this book.) David Clyde fell into my lap while all national media outlets were chasing him. (*Sports Illustrated *caught him before that fall, but the Boston Globe was still interested in my approach to the story.)*

Pittsfield—A sequel to "David Clyde, Anointed Adolescent."

In which a 6-foot-1, curly-haired 18-year-old lad compiled a magnificent high school pitching record, graduated from his Houston school; signed, in 1973, a six-figure baseball contract with the home state Rangers; made his major league debut a fortnight and a half later, before an unprecedented full house (10,000 folks were turned away); and, with the eyes of Texas and the Almighty upon him, became the winning pitcher that night.

In which young David became: "a dream come true," according to the mayor of Arlington, Texas; a Goliath-nemesis, according to the press; an authentic savior, according to many Texans and some ordinary people; an all-too-human sacrifice, according to a Paul-Bunyan-fistful of skeptics; a husband to a high school companion, according to the vows exchanged.

In which Bob Short, then owner of the Texas team, was castigated by many for using—abusing—David Clyde in order to save a franchise.

In which a few people counter-contended that the true 'villain' was J.E. Clyde, the prodigy's father, who, these few alleged, had established the immediacy of his son's big league appearance in a contractual stipulation.

In which the young pitcher devoted more time to watching than to pitching through the two summers spent as a major leaguer, working a total of 210 innings, during which he gave up an average of more than four and one-half runs for every nine of those innings, recording 7 victories while losing 17 games, a layer of glitter and immeasurable self-confidence.

So ended Book One.

What had begun as a contemporary fairy tale concluded as hard-core realism. Quite a different genre.

The sequel begins this spring in Pittsfield (yes, Pittsfield), Massachusetts. Quite a different setting. The Pittsfield Rangers are having their season-opening banquet in friendly, albeit modest, surroundings offered by the Highland Restaurant, a local spot. This Rangers team is the AA Eastern League affiliate of the parent Texas club.

Twenty-one young minor leaguers are present. David Clyde is among them, endearing himself to townies. In return for these local folks' enthusiastic greetings and introductions of self, Clyde offers, without demur, a terse, "Glad to meet you, sir (or ma'am)" and a tight handshake. It is model New England manners for a young 'un, as the numerous nods of Yankee approval confirm. The Southwesterner's twang seems to go unnoticed.

Courtesy, tact and respect for elders are not recent acquisitions of this just-turned-20-year-old. The traits were clearly manifest during frequent dealings with media men, way back when. In this respect, he has not changed.

What has changed, obviously, is David Clyde's physical and personal environments, both a long haul from 'Big T.' But also evident is a corollary permutation—a resultant overhaul of the young man's self, which began during the weeks of recuperation from a February tonsillectomy. The physical respite (during the winter he had played ball in Venezuela) provided sufficient time for an active and conscientious struggle with his persona.

A dramatic monologue serves best here.

"They used to call me an All-American boy. Now, because of a divorce, some people think I'm controversial. But I've never fit that 'All-American' image. I'm just an ordinary kid who hit a lucky once-in-a-million chance, and who doesn't want to be something he's not.

"I realize that the public is interested in athletes and entertainers, that they want to know about you. But they have to realize that you're human too. My marriage didn't work out, and I know it was my fault. I had plenty of time to think about it after the operation. I understood myself better: in the last few months I've changed an awful lot. I'm becoming more of an introvert now.

"I also realize that it would have been better for me to start off in the minors. My pitching has been set back a couple of years. With all that was going on around me in the majors, I couldn't concentrate the way I did in high school. The curve ball would work fine on the sidelines, then, in a game, I'd get the ball back to here (a gesture illustrates the throwing position, hand poised behind the ear) and something says to me, 'You can't throw a curve.' The curve was the pitch I threw most in high school. Everybody wrote I was a fastball pitcher, but the curve was my best pitch.

"That's what I'm here in Pittsfield for. That and my change of pace (un-intentional double-meaning there). Actually, I'm glad to be here. Now I can act my age. I used to be an 18-year-old trying to act like a 30-year-old, but I'm relaxed now; I feel good about everything. My life has slowed down; my head is on straighter. Everyone said that I handled the pressure up there so well, but I never felt that way. At least, not when I was on the mound.

"I still want to be a great pitcher—the greatest. I don't want to be the kid who went right to the big leagues and didn't make it.

"As I said, I'm a different person. I know I'll make it."

So ended the monologue.

A part of the metamorphosis was apparent that night in the Highland's relaxed social milieu. Seated next to teammates Bump Wills (Maury's boy) and a bright-eyed third baseman whose blonds curls cascaded from his five-foot, eight-inch summit, and whose improbable name is Gary Cooper, the new David Clyde quietly spoke about matters on which young men are wont to converse: an aversion for peas and crème de menthe trickling over a ball of vanilla ice cream in such a way as to give it the appearance of "A Martian's bloodshot eye," college courses (David had attended Texas A&M for a spell in winter, '73), journalism, insurance and a variety of lighter considerations.

At the same time one handsome and affable Jackie Moore, age 36, was completing his repast at another table. Though played inconspicuously, his has been an important role in the ongoing saga. You see, he is the recently-appointed manager of the Pittsfield Rangers.

That's not all. Called "the nicest man in professional baseball" by at least one current American League player, Moore had been a coach with Clyde's Texas team before the managerial appointment, had scouted his prized Pittsfield pitcher when the boy was in high school, had accompanied him to Venezuela the winter past, and just happens to be from Houston himself. An executive finger writes, and having writ, moves on.

In essence, Moore has become David Clyde's alter ego. Old enough to be the dispenser of life's verities, young enough to communicate them clearly to his charge, Moore is, in addition, good-natured enough to be a pleasant companion and firm enough to be a responsible guardian. Further, he is the manager and, not least, please remember, a Texan.

Moore reviewed the past. "I guess it could be said that David saved the Texas franchise. We had a bad ball club and there was little interest before he came on the scene. I don't think Bo Short was sacrificing him though. He was gambling, hoping for some luck, in the same way he did with Jeff Burroughs and Vic Harris."

Well now, the record shows that Burroughs played in the minor leagues exclusively during his first professional year and was shuttled back and forth during his next three years. His experience chart shows 995 at-bats in the minors as opposed to only 258 at-bats with 'the big club' during that period. Not until 1973 did Burroughs become a regular major league outfielder. In 1974 he fulfilled his physical promise and became a celebrity in baseball circles—five years after his professional debut.

Harris, on the other hand, played two years in the minors, came to Texas in a trade, participated in 61 games, hitting at an average below his weight when wet—.170. He performed as a regular the next season, batted .249, was traded to Chicago in the National League, where he spent most of the 1974 season—on the disabled list.

Hardly a good luck story in Harris's case; hardly an acceptable analogy in either case.

However, there is no disparity between Moore's words and those articulated by David Clyde. Always the themes are parallel; occasionally there is a facsimile of wording. The identity of the script writer is not important. Player and manager seem to believe in their pronouncement, which include references to a Venezuelan winter's 1-3 pitching record ("I/He was only there to work on certain pitches"), the curve ball ("It should be my/his best pitch"), the mental approach to the game ("The important things are concentration and confidence").

Moore is adamant in his gentlemanly way about a point of great import to the organization. "David is not here in Pittsfield to prove he can pitch. We all *know* he can do that. He is here to get in a lot of innings—experience. To bring his curve ball from the sidelines into the game."

Moore went on: "His attitude is realistic; his feelings aren't hurt. It just might be a good thing for him, having been up there already. He sees now what it takes. He's got to throw strikes with his curve ball, so they can't dig in and wait to hit the fast ball. That's what they did, and he knows all about that."

David Clyde will know more about things come September. But experience, as Oscar Wilde pointed out, is one thing you can't get for nothing. A down payment has already been made. Pittsfield's Opening Day was postponed due to abominable conditions in the atmosphere and on the playing field. Just as well, perhaps. At David's debut in Texas, the Arlington mayor, a happy if hyperbolic fellow, proclaimed that time there would henceforth be marked from the date of that illustrious event. Pittsfield's mayor, when invited to throw out the first pitch at his town's Clyde Bash, proclaimed he was playing in a tennis tournament and couldn't make it, thank you, could he send his wife?

Conditions the next day were somewhat improved for a time. And the mayor could sling it. But meteorological matters became worse than they had been the previous day. Meanwhile, in the locker room, all the players were snuggled in their fresh long johns and double knits. All except—you guessed it—David Clyde. His uniform couldn't be found, or was locked in a trunk, or some such inanity. Pacing the bare concrete floor of the ever-so-slow-to-warm room, the starting pitcher for the day turned his mind to the slimy cold outside.

He drew himself together for warmth against the thought and, addressing no one in particular, muttered, "In the majors they have heated dugouts."

Coach Marty Martinez was close enough to hear the innocent remark and willing enough to spear it. With a wide outward sweep of his arms and with an even wider grin, he bowed low in pantomime of courtly obeisance and offered his response: "Welcome to the minor leagues, David Clyde."

So ended Book Two.

Moments later the game was canceled. Book Three, "Another Opening, Another Show," begins this way: A 2-0 loss to Three Rivers (Quebec) despite eight strikeouts: a 2-0 win over Quebec City, with thirteen strikeouts.

Much more will be written.

Postscript—David Clyde's major league pitching statistics included 18 wins and 33 losses. His earned run average was 4.63. Clyde pitched his final big league game in 1979. He was 24 years old.

Hall-of-Fame manager Whitey Herzog, who managed Clyde in 1973, said that he regretted going along with Bob Short's desire to rush a young kid to the major leagues. Herzog said he was forced to leave Clyde in games longer than was appropriate—or normal—for a young pitcher because fans wanted to see the 18-year-old "phenom" pitch. He believes that helped cause Clyde's arm problems.

Clyde, in later years, expressed his own belief that he was rushed too early in his career. He said philosophically, "If nothing else came out of my career, the things I hear periodically are, 'We're not gonna do to that young man what we did to David Clyde.'"

Steven Strasburg, perhaps, is the beneficiary of that willful point of view.

17

You Get the Message?

The Manchester Journal, July 24, 1975

A conversation with a faculty colleague frustrated and perplexed me. An understanding of the issue we were discussing was never reached: the classic 'semantic argument.' Having an academic background in semantics, I was especially frustrated by my inability to make the other party "see clearly"—as I said to her. Could it be that I was not seeing clearly? Of course not.

In any case, it made me think about language: its uses and effects—some amusing, some not. Nothing too profound, surely, but provocative enough to move me to write something about the communication process and the complications language brings to that process.

And just for the record—Semantics: fr. the Greek word semantikos, *meaning 'significant.' Semantics is the study of meanings and of behavior in reaction to non-verbal and verbal symbols (words).*

During a discussion of language and communication held two weeks ago, a number of folks, myself included, agreed—more or less—that language is the dress of thought. We didn't follow up with any extensional considerations at the time, but it now strikes me that I also believe 'clothes do *not* make the man.' A tedious point to pursue, particularly in today's heat.

However, it might be worthwhile to reacquaint ourselves with the fact that interpersonal communication is not to be taken for granted. Very often we are frustrated by a mutual lack of understanding. More often we think we *do* understand someone else's thoughts—as expressed through his words—when, in actuality, we have misunderstood the message as it was intended. Recognizing the guilty party is no easy matter, nor is it of much value after the fact.

What we must recognize before we communicate with one another is the possibility (probability?) that our common words may not trigger the same image in someone else's mind as they do in our own. Realizing this, we can improve our 'system' of being as specific as possible in the way we use words. If we ask questions of the speaker, the likelihood of greater clarity increases. Even then we may fall one question short.

The importance of proper use of language to the communicative process was clearly and seriously established for me some years ago by a couple of stodgy fellows named Marckwardt and Walcott in their *Facts About Current English Usage.* Improper usage, I've since discovered, has its lighter side. To support this contention a yellowed and frayed sheet has been resurrected from my filing cabinet. I've seen copies of it around recently and so, perhaps, has the reader. Included on the paper are sixteen sentences taken from actual letters received by one of the agencies in a large city. The letters were sent in application for financial support. (The requests were serious enough.) Though the intentions of the applicants are identical, the explanations of need are diverse and distinctive. (Only nine of them are listed below in consideration of advertisers' similar need for self-expression on this page.)

- I am writing your department to say that my baby was born two years old. When do I get the money?
- Mrs. Jones has not had any clothes for a year and has been visited regularly by the clergy.
- I cannot get sick pay. I have six children. Can you tell me why?
- This is my eighth child. What are you going to do about it?
- Please find for certain if my husband is dead. The man I am now living with can't eat or do anything until he knows.
- I am very much annoyed to find that you have branded my boy illiterate. This is a dirty lie. As I married a week before he was born.
- I am forwarding my marriage certificate and my three children, one of which is a mistake, as you can see.
- You changed my boy to a girl. Will this make any difference?
- In accordance with your instruction, I have given birth to twins in the enclosed envelope.

We are all hard put to make sense out of sound from time to time. Some of us have shorter time spans than others. But even when language is used impeccably, we assume too much, believing to know exactly what others are talking about or presuming that everyone else knows exactly what we are talking about.

A psychiatrist story best illustrates this propensity.

Having been greeted by a fellow shrink's, "Good morning," the first psychiatrist paused and queried himself: "I wonder what he means by that?"

It might be useful for us all to remember that question—and to direct it at more opportune times and on more appropriate occasions.

18

Woman Umpire Story: The Perils of Christine

The New York Times, August 17, 1975

"Baseball, hot dogs, apple pie and Chevrolet." So went the jingle years ago, the branch of General Motors confirming itself as an All-American staple.

As a freelance writer, I was often hard-put to come up with ideas for articles. No one called me and asked for my work. When I did have an idea, I had to go through the standard query-procedure as presented to such as me by The Writer's Market.

So, when I had the thought that a piece on a young woman umpire might be of interest to someone, I thought immediately of the Chevy house organ—the magazine the automobile folks called Friends.

I, myself, had umpired high school and college games for eleven years. The value of that, I thought, would be greater for persuading the young woman to do the piece with me than it would for the magazine to say, "Yes." As it turned out, both agreed to my scheme.

I flew to Boise, Idaho, in June, 1975, and traveled with Christine Wren in her van for a week, as she made her professional debut in the Northwest (Rookie) League. The Chevy magazine ran a full interview (question and answer format) and many pictures (including the one on its cover).

This format allowed me to write a related article with a different slant—one that The New York Times *was, according to the editor, happy to run. They did so in August, 1975. (Because of lead time that magazines require when publishing, the interview in* Friends *ran in 1976.)*

Much of the Times *piece speaks of Christine's predecessor in pro baseball, a woman who made it harder, rather than easier, for Christine to be a credible figure on the baseball field.*

Part of America's sports mania is its preoccupation with "being No. 1," both directly (through participation) and vicariously (through spectatorship). The need for this often-excessive absorption, planted in remote historical ground, has germinated, sprouted, blossomed and borne fruit which, spreading over the years, has crept into the continent's fields like a national cucumber.

And now, a somewhat tangential issue of primacy has been raised with the advent of Christine Wren, the second woman to have become a professional baseball umpire. Her appearance on the baseball scene, noted for its own uniqueness, has, in addition, revived interest in Bernice Gera, Miss Wren's predecessor and affixer of "First Woman Umpire" under her signature.

Along with this revival comes the consideration of 'first' as opposed to 'best,' or precedent as the embalmer of principle. In this regard, Mrs. Gera has been given a low score by many of baseball's contemporary historians.

But history is no more than biography, and the basic element of biography—an individual's singular character and motivations, and the consequent circumstances—can best obviate the matter of Mrs. Gera's numerical and numerological significance.

In 1972, after close to four years of legal battles, Bernice Gera made her professional umpiring debut in the Class A New York-Pennsylvania League. Working the bases as part of a two-person crew, Mrs. Gera, not without incident (she threw one of the managers out of the game after a heated argument stemming from her reversed decision at second base), completed her work in the first game of a scheduled double-header and called it a career. She announced to a swarm of media folk in the clubhouse that she had "just resigned from baseball." She then left to allow her tears to wash the egg and splattered bubble from her face.

Chauvinists and cynics marked that date; baseball "purists" have held her in low esteem since. (One wonders if they ever held her anywhere else.) Needless to say, she was labeled "quitter," the No. 1 sports blasphemy. Further, her contribution of "paving the way" for other female umpiring aspirants has been demeaned.

The road to the warm place is paved with good intentions, the demeanors say, and therein rests a contradiction, part of the answer for those objective enough to consider Mrs. Gera an enigma, at worst. Like Christine Wren, Bernice Gera had developed a love of baseball by age 8; like Christine Wren, she played professional women's softball; like Christine Wren, she knew the position of the doors to baseball's hallowed Hall of Men.

Unlike Christine Wren, she was the one who first battered and ultimately broke down one of those doors. Mrs. Gera's original aspiration—intention, if you will—was to become part, any part, of baseball's world. ("I would have shined players' shoes, had they let me," she still insists.) Christine Wren's exclusive goal is to become a major league umpire.

Though both of their 'behaviors' must be examined in light of these intentions, the fact remains that Mrs. Gera did open the door. But to what? Christine Wren admits to little knowledge of Bernice Gera's experience. Nevertheless, Miss Wren feels that her own early umpiring experiences, in school and on the playing fields, were made more difficult because her seriousness of purpose—her credibility—was questioned.

Others' recollections of Miss Wren's 'predecessor' hung over her like a stale vapor. Many still see it hovering there. But the darkest part of an umpire's eye cannot perceive the true nature of the vapor's substance.

The differences between the women—their placement in time, their chemistry and physiology, their age, their knowledge, even their male umpiring partners (Gad, what a difference there!)—their whole being, may some day be revealed to pundits, minor and mediocre. For according to Luke, "Nothing is secret that shall not be made manifest."

Meanwhile, the time is right for the revelation of some secret and honest details, according to Mrs. Gera. Her original goal realized, she is now "happy beyond words" as a member of the New York Mets' public relations department.

Within the security of the better bubble she has built, Bernice Gera now admits that her bags were packed before that first day on the job. ("I decided to quit before I went out there. I was tired of fighting.") She would "think twice" before going through the whole business again.

There are "a few notes" she has kept from those days—accounts and, one hopes, perceptions—causes. The effects, Mrs. Gera should realize, will not accurately speak for themselves. Perhaps, as she says, she will yet decide to write about it all.

Suffice to say, Christine Wren, her first bubble thus far intact, will be writing a considerably different story. In each case, lest you forget, it will be called biography. And that can be much more nourishing than cucumber.

19

Books, Children and Parents

The Manchester Journal, December 18, 1975

This was to be the last column I would write for the local newspaper. The Rutland Herald, *a state paper published 25 miles north of Manchester, became interested in the possibility of my writing a weekly column for their Thursday 'Vermont Living Section.' I'd done plenty of sports coverage and features for them, and now they thought I should expand my vistas. I told them I had written a column for years. (They apparently didn't read the Journal.) OK, they said, so expand your vista to our pages. I accepted. The motivation? A larger audience would be reached. A larger paycheck would be realized.*

So I climbed onto my Manchester soapbox and spewed out some final words on a subject very important to me—as an individual, as a father and as an educator.

(No such things as twittering and texting in that world. Still not—in mine.)

There's nothing new about it, really. Children learn from models, and we are those models. What we *say* means more to us than to them. What we *do* sets the example. And there is often little new about what we do. Creatures of habit, you might say; some habits more exemplary than others. But we do have high ideals for the young folks. They'll know; they'll do.

Take reading. We tell children how "important" it is to know how to read. Do we tell them it's a joy? *Is* it a joy to us? Do they listen, or do they watch? Do we just talk, or do we act?

Recently, a group of 100 fourth, fifth and sixth graders, through the process of interview, revealed that, though most children develop their ability to read in school, the home and family "are a greater influence in the development of reading habits."

Linda Lamme, assistant professor of Early Childhood Education at the University of Florida, conducted a three-year study of those 100 children. She found that every avid reader in the group came from a home where there was at least one adult who read regularly. Yet, "many children whose parents read widely did not enjoy reading themselves. But the children who are readers unanimously agree that their parents' reading habits influence their own."

I have told this before. My own father was a man whose verbal link of communication with his only son was sporadically used. Nevertheless I am left with many strong images of him. I remember the back of his head vividly. As a boy, I stopped to look at it often, while en route to my room. The still head would be just visible over the high back of his cushioned chair. I'd sneak a stare from the side every so often, when I was feeling courageous. Disturbance meant danger. There, transcending the modest environs of his apartment's living room, he sat—reading. He took occasional puffs on a pipe from which no smoke ever seemed to rise. What magic, I thought. That this man can be so peaceful, so satisfied.

Surely, I tried it one day. The chair was oversized and uncomfortable; the pipe bitter; the book (*Mary* by Sholem Asch sticks in my head) beyond comprehension. But all that was external only. The internal mattered to me then and remains significant to me now. I had decided to love reading by the time I pushed myself out of the vastness of that chair.

Models, however, are not always enough. Professor Lamme's earlier comments indicate as much. Overt parental action can help. The children involved in the study gave examples of parental policy which affected their interest in reading.

- Regular use of the town library.
- Reading when and where the children observed the parent.
- Reading favorite passages aloud.
- Giving books as gifts.
- Discussing what is read with other family members.
- Providing some book space for each child.
- Enjoying listening to children read aloud.
- Reading aloud to children regularly.

We can each think of others, some more suitable for our own family circumstances perhaps. And no guarantees are inherent in the attempts we make. But consider this: After six years of formal schooling, a youngster has spent only seven percent of his life in school. At age eleven then (assuming an age five start), 93 percent of the child's time has been spent outside of school. That seems to present quite a responsibility for all of us, as parents and as models.

No, there's nothing new about it really, though it just might be worth remembering from time to time. And before we tell our children how important it is to read, we might also remember that the man who *does not* read had no advantage over the man who *cannot* read. The children will watch, the children will know.

Postscript—How the world has changed since 1975. How we have changed.

20

Christine Wren: Another Season

The New York Times, June 6, 1976

The Times *was interested in a Christine Wren (woman umpire) follow-up. Christine had done better than all the chauvinists predicted. (Could she have done worse? Well, Bernice Gera had.) So they ran my sequel, based on the fact that she would work again in a second year. And years later, another woman appeared on the umpiring scene. I was by then the voice of women's baseball arbiters. The third ump was named Pam Postema. The Boston Herald American ran my feature in 1979. It is not included in this volume: wretched excess.*

What is *included—as a postscript—is a Midwest new release in the form of a short 'biography' of Christine Wren. It is useful, I think, to those who have an interest in a more defined picture of Christine Wren's umpiring experience. My piece presents some of the reaction to Miss Wren during her first season.*

Several weeks ago, excerpts from two books about baseball and black Americans appeared on this page. Their sociologically specific point should have been clear to every reader. Interestingly enough, both statements concluded with references to baseball and the American woman who is still a minority of one.

Christine Wren remains the exclusive representative of that gender on the playing fields of Organized Baseball today. This month she will begin her second season as a professional umpire, returning to the short-season Class A Northwest League.

Ecclesiastes notwithstanding, Miss Wren's appearance last year was something new under the sun—and lights. And it should come as no surprise that, human nature being what it is, the novelty was at times handled with little grace and less style.

Many people had much to say before, during and after Miss Wren's precedent-setting first season. Poverty of wit, the idiom of the trade, relative objectivity, a hint of compassion, among other things, may be discerned in the following sampling.

- January, 1975 (at the Specialized Umpire Training Course in Mission Hills, California). "I had to fight to get at the mechanical equipment. Everyone was afraid I'd get hurt."—Christine Wren
- April, 1975. The suggestion is made that "women don't have the guts to be major league umpires."—Chris Pelekoudas, former major league umpire (male).
- June 17, 1975. "I'm here because I want to be a major league umpire."—Christine Wren.
- June 17, 1975. "I didn't hire her as a publicity stunt."—Bob Richmond, league president.
- June 18, 1975. "Why on earth does a nice-looking broad like that want to be an umpire?"—Gary Winklebauer, Portland Mavericks pitcher.
- June 19, 1975. "She's a fine person."—Ron Scott, Portland Mavericks catcher.
- June 19, 1975. "She's got to be a masochist."—Unidentified Boise A's player.
- June 22, 1975. "Go home and do the laundry, Chris!"—Male spectator in Walla Walla, Washington.
- June 22, 1975. "Hang in there, Chrissy!"—Female spectator in Walla Walla, Washington.
- June 23, 1975. "She does O.K., but O.K. won't be good enough for a babe. Chris can't be good or better. She's got to be the best. She's not yet, and I don't know if she ever will be. But she's got a cute bottom, doesn't she?"—Frank Peters, manager of the Portland Mavericks.
- July 12, 1975. "She's got a lot to learn. She's done a good job in the arguments she's been in; she isn't afraid to throw a player out, but she doesn't yet understand when she should or shouldn't. She hasn't shown much improvement on the bases. Her motions are a little bit more aggressive, but her judgment is still shaky. I realize it takes more than one year to develop, but physically, I don't think she can cut a long season."—Gary Lieberman, Miss Wren's umpiring partner. *(A pal? Not.)*
- July, 1975. "You worked a fine game."—Jim Bouton to Christine Wren, who umpired behind the plate the night of Bouton's return to professional baseball. Pitching for the Portland Mavericks, he went all the way for a 5-3 victory.
- September, 1975. "I admire her for her determination, but I don't think she has what it takes to be a major league umpire."—Gary Lieberman, after the season, which Miss Wren completed without missing a game, despite having had her collarbone broken by a foul ball and having lost the feeling in her fingers weeks later after being hit in the arm by another foul tip.
- October, 1975. "I learned an awful lot, and one of the things I learned was how much more I still have to master. It was a huge experience, and not one any male umpire has ever had. I didn't pack my bags and go home; some men did. I finished. There were plenty of people who didn't think I'd make it through one-third of the season. Bernice Gera lasted one day. It just proves that other people's opinions are irrelevant. I'm going to keep working hard. I hope to get the promotion I think I deserve. Gary Lieberman was a big help, but sometimes

he was over-protective. I'm not used to that. I think that's the attitude he has toward women, and that didn't help me the way he thought it would. I think Gary doesn't like to give credit to women for being able to take care of themselves and do well."—Christine Wren.

- January, 1976. "Christine Wren will again be working in the Class A Northwest League from the middle of June through August. It's nothing unusual. There are only three rookie umpires in that league this year. Lieberman has moved up to a longer-season Class A league after three years in the Northwest. There's not so much force-feeding umpires any more. We'd rather season them."—Barney Deary, Administrator of Umpire Development.
- April, 1976. "I think they're trying to hold me down."—Christine Wren.
- Circa 1860. "Time will teach more than all our thoughts."—Benjamin Disraeli.

Postscript—A Midwest League Release after the 1977 season.

The Midwest League's (full-season, Class A) umpire staff included Christine Wren, age 27, from Spokane and Seattle.

1977 was Wren's third professional season; she worked in the Northwest League during the previous two summers. She'd also worked in spring training for two years, though she'd not been invited to participate in the 1977 spring. In 1975, she'd umpired a Dodgers-Southern Cal exhibition game before 51,000 baseball fans.

Wren's umpiring received general good reviews, even from those who didn't approve of a woman ump. According to most reports, she was an excellent ball-and-strike umpire; as a basepath umpire, it was claimed she needed some work. It was also reported that her basepath work improved from year to year. Some baseball men, including Barney Deary, Baseball Umpire Development administrator, expressed concerns about her stamina which, quite frankly, read like sexism.

Wren's Midwest League season (1977) was a success. MWL President Bill Walters consistently said positive things about her performance, and selected her to umpire the 1977 MWL All-Star Game that summer.

Bill Walters invited Wren to return in 1978. Instead, she took a leave of absence, and never returned. She'd become convinced that organized ball wouldn't give her an opportunity to succeed.

The press coverage of Wren's career was fascinating. An amazing proportion of it has to be called condescending, casting Wren as a "girl" in a profession of worldly men. It's quite clear that she learned the hard way that she couldn't tell reporters everything she believed. By her MWL summer, she was pretty careful about what she said and who she talked to. H.A. Dorfman, a college prof and former umpire who followed Wren's career for The New York Times, *stands out as a balanced and sympathetic reporter.*

21

Casey Stengel, Facts and Much Fiction

The New York Times, September 26, 1976

I've always been interested in the disparity between perception and reality. Especially as it relates to public figures. After years of being around professional athletes, who certainly are such figures—celebrities, if you will—my interest has waned. But at the time of this writing, I was still stimulated by the phenomenon. The images mass man has created of these prominent figures would make, by comparison, police composite drawings look like photos taken by a Canon SD700.

The readership's reaction to the piece was interesting—and predictable. I was berated and chastised in letters to the editor—and to me—by those who were offended in Stengel's behalf. Did they read the article carefully? An irrelevant question, I suppose. Whatever the case may have been, a number of pejorative terms were hooked on me. One woman called me "a moron." I'd been called many things in my years, a lout on numerous occasions, but until the Stengel piece, never a "moron."

O.K., understood. Still, I was heartened by a note from Frank Litsky, my editor at The Times. *In it he said, "It was the kind of story that someone should have done long ago, but no one did." Maybe they couldn't handle the inevitable abuse.*

Casey Stengel has been dead for a year. It is harsh to say, but everyone seems to agree that that's what he is. In itself, this is a kind of enlightened thinking. After all, not every legend has been allowed to die.

Casey Stengel arrived in the Bronx to manage the Yankees simultaneous to my arrival at a Bronx high school. Neither arrival produced much fanfare, but Stengel won a pennant and World Series in his freshman year there, while I finished far off the pace of clackety-teeth lectures in mythology class. Kerkis, Rudens and Rhesis intrigued me less than Kerr, Rizzuto and Reese. Twenty-seven years later, Stengel and mythology have conjoined in an intrigue of coincidence.

WHAT A MAN!

Stengel's death precipitated specious eulogies, retrospective anecdotes and post-obituary "disclosures," most of which conspired to obscure reality, which in itself is a sliding door.

During the last year the man has been referred to as a joker and a clowning loser, a Socrates and an original, a public clown but not a private one. He wasn't playing the fool even when sliding on hotel lobby floors, said one news periodical. He almost always made sense even when people laughed at him. He wasn't lovable at all, it went on. A West Coast newspaper said he was so.

Other sources have provided labels such as master psychologist, Merlin, gadfly, gargoyle, a combination of Donald Duck and Charles de Gaulle. Gov. Hugh Carey offered his own composite Casey: "the mind of a genius, the heart of Santa Claus and St. Francis, the face of a clown."

Stengel began his baseball career near-crazy, according to a popular story of his. As a minor league player en route to his defensive position he would often practice sliding—on the outfield grass. This apparent mental infirmity worried his manager, his teammates or the clinician in the "lunatic asylum" outside the outfield fence, depending on whose story you've heard or read.

Stengelians have relished and embellished similar anecdotes so as to assure the public that, until age 59, Charles Stengel was a "certified buffoon" with little else to commend himself. "He began decrepit and grew younger," it has been written. Yet his .284 for 14 major league seasons and .393 average for three World Series are real, if little regarded, statistics—remarkable, actually, for one with such premature infirmities. In truth, the fans he made as a big league player respected the ability denied him by the many media people who mythicized him.

Brooklyn fans loved him particularly. These same fans, disappointed by his trade to Pittsburgh during the winter of 1917, heckled him when he made his first 1918 appearance in Flatbush. The ensuing event augmented the grand distortion. Casey tipped his cap to the faithful and everything from pigeons to biplanes were to have flown out of that cap. It was a sparrow, caught by Brooklyn pitcher, Leon Cadore, who presented it to his pal and former teammate. The bird was put to immediate use. So was the story.

Stengel's managerial career gained him the most acclaim. His reputation as a magician stemmed from his Yankees' ten pennants and seven World Series championships in 12 seasons. Yet Stengel himself understood the irony of "transformation" after his poor managerial results in Brooklyn and Boston.

TRUTH IS STRONGER …

A former major league coach, Clyde Sukeforth, recalls Stengel asking Billy Meyers, then manager of the hapless Pirates, "How come you got so dumb and I got so smart?" Needless to say, it was a rhetorical question.

Still, clever rhetoriticians had their way after Stengel's death, writing of his early managerial failures: "His initial triumphs were negative." A tongue in glory's cheek.

An "amusing" and frequently-referred-to truth from those early days is that the Dodgers paid him *not* (affect a smug laugh when emphasizing this word) to manage (40 years ago next week). Unusual? Alvin Dark, Chuck Tanner, Dick Williams, Darrell Johnson, *et. al.* wouldn't think so. Max Carey, Stengel's predecessor, was treated similarly, down to the salary paid off—$13,000. You could look it up, as everyone likes to say that Stengel liked to say.

Tales from the successful Yankee era offer no singularly penetrating glimpses into the man. Surely, the clown became the Old Perfessor, who miraculously platooned the right players, played the right hunches, hunched against the faulty percentages. The players who played the most expressed appreciation by calling him a masterful juggler; the infrequent platoonees depreciated a lucky bumbler.

The year after being summarily stripped of his genius by the Yankee brass, who had originally hired him to fill the role of a crowd-pleasing distraction, Stengel was hired by the original Mets. Players said their manager could often be found amazingly asleep in the dugout during games. Some blamed senility; some credited good sense.

Stengel never used a player's name, the fella now managing the Yankees recalled. He rarely used the right one, a current Mets coach clarifies.

"Mythology," wrote Ambrose Bierce, "is the body of primitive peoples' beliefs concerning heroes, deities and so forth, as distinguished from the true accounts, which it invents later."

22

Things Have Gone Real Well for Floyd Patterson

The Rutland Herald, October 10, 1976

It was with enthusiastic anticipation that I approached doing a feature story for the Herald's *Sunday sports section. Floyd Patterson was coming to Vermont (barely crossing the Massachusetts border) and the paper wanted to take advantage of the former heavyweight champion's presence in the state.*

In 1961, less than a year after Anita and I had married and moved into our home in Commack, New York, Patterson fought Ingemar Johansson in the rubber match of a three-fight face-off. I remember well having purchased a ticket—$10!—to watch the fight on closed-circuit TV at Commack Arena. (We were both teaching; no children yet, so I splurged.)

Anita had mild interest, since Johansson was a Swede—the first from his country to ever become a heavyweight champion when he won the first meeting in June, 1959. The ref stopped the fight in the third round after Patterson had gone down seven times. Patterson won the 1960 rematch, becoming the first man to regain the undisputed heavyweight title.

The fight I witnessed at Commack Arena was held in March, 1961. I remember thinking I had wasted my money when Patterson hit the canvas twice in the first round. But Johansson was decked once in the same round—and Patterson went on to win the fight in by a knockout in the 6th.

My greatest interest in interviewing Patterson, however, came from a desire to hear for myself the man who so confounded the boxing pundits of the world—the 'inside' men and the media. Here was a fighter who did not want to hurt his opponent. I was reminded of the story of the Quaker who had a score to settle with a local fellow. As he held his musket at the ready, he said to the man who had wronged him, "I would not harm thee for the world, but thou standeth where I shoot."

I could hear Patterson saying to an opponent in the ring, "I would not hurt thee for the world, but thou standeth where I punch."

One media wag, whose literary reach was well short of his grasp, called Patterson the "Heavyweight Hamlet," confusing introversion with introspection. Patterson's shyness was uncomplicated; he may not have known what 'to be,' but he was clear on what 'not to be.'

And, more the fun, I would bring my Swedish wife along to meet a guy who, based on the relationship he developed with Johansson, had spent time living in Sweden—and loved the country.

Pownal, Vt.—Twenty-seven years, 64 fights and 10 million dollars ago, Floyd Patterson began a boxing career. He was 15 at the time, and his mother didn't like the idea. The boy, she said, was too timid for that sort of stuff.

At 16, the boy became a Golden Gloves champion; at 17 he won an Olympic gold medal; at 21 he was crowned world heavyweight champion—the youngest ever; at 24 he was a dethroned champion—the youngest ever; at 27 he lost his title forever; at 37, no longer a boy, he fought and lost to Muhammad Ali (Patterson still calls him Cassius Clay). It was Patterson's last fight, though at the time he said he wanted to continue boxing as long as he could.

"I'm still in it," he says with a smile.

Last week a 42-year-old 'new man' brought a troupe of young fighters from the Hugenot Club in New Paltz, New York, to Green Mountain Race Track in Pownal, for a card of six amateur matches. His role as teacher, trainer and second is, in Patterson's words, "greatly satisfying." But this satisfaction may be incomprehensible to many of those who still care to monkey with the man's often-discussed psychological clockwork.

In the jockey's room below the track, Patterson was busy and happy, a hint of smugness in his manner. His gears seemed well-oiled, and he ticked easily and regularly.

"I'm content now," he said as he wrapped the hand of the first Hugenot Club fighter. Patterson raised his dark eyes to punctuate the import of his remark. "I never knew what I wanted; I probably still don't. But who knows?" he asked rhetorically. "At least I knew what I didn't want."

He repeated the interviewer's question. "What was it I didn't want? It was what a heavyweight champion was forced to be—was obligated to do: to be a public figure, in the spotlight, making public appearances, traveling all over the world, meeting people. I hated it, and I couldn't do it. I always admired Ingemar Johansson after he took the title away from me. He did all that and loved it. I wished at the time that I could."

Patterson's eyes went up to the room's elevated television set. Heavyweight Duane Bobich was administering a pounding to Chuck Wepner. Someone in the room said Wepner was the perfect opponent for Bobich, that is, he was a big, slow-moving target.

Then another camp follower came over and told Patterson the name of the fellow refereeing the televised match. Patterson, becoming animated, turned to his visitor and asked, again rhetorically, "You remember the Ellis fight I had in Sweden? Well, that guy up there (a nod toward the TV set) was the ref. Ellis's manager, Angelo Dundee, brought that guy over with them. I didn't find out about it until after the fight."

Patterson lost that fight on a controversial decision, but he never uttered a public complaint. "The referee decides," he said at the time. "I have nothing to say about the decision. I do not wish to detract from Jimmy's fight." He said he was also sorry he had "busted his (Jimmy Ellis's) nose" during the fight. It was the kind of gesture—restraint and passivity, in this case—that became his hallmark. Many critics, particularly men of the press, found fault with his gentleness. They concocted stories which the former heavyweight champion still shakes his head over.

Yet admitted facts about behavior uncharacteristic of heavyweight boxers are enough to raise an eyebrow or two.

Fact: Patterson used to say, "My opponent is a guy with feelings like me. I'd rather win on a decision than a knockout." (40 of his 55 victories were KO's.)

Fact: Patterson wore numerous disguises when leaving arenas, often when traveling, in order to avoid attention. (His most grotesque was the five-and-dime store false nose, eyeglasses and moustache.)

Fact: Five years ago, before his final fight, against Ali, Patterson said, "My goal isn't to become champion again." What he wanted—besides the fat purse—was "to improve."

Fact: Floyd Patterson has used his boxing money wisely and is now a wealthy man. And now, he says, a healthy man, as well.

Years ago one boxing writer, assessing the causes of Patterson's unpredictability in the ring, said, "It all depends on his state of mind. For a long period he fought as if he were trying to recall an old dance step, and his mind wandered."

The fighter himself offered his own commentary last week. "I was mostly a moody fighter. Sometimes I couldn't get psyched up. The writers always added something to it. They said something was wrong up here." He tapped his temple and grinned broadly.

What they said were things such as, "Patterson (is) the Captain Ahab of boxing who, many think, should retire and cultivate his neuroses."

They said he was an anti-hero; they said the Swedes loved him not—as they claimed—for his gentleness, but rather because they related to his melancholia. They said he was tormented, and they said he fought too many bad fighters. They even said Ali was kind to him in that last bout in '72. Kind to a 37-year-old man who didn't know when to quit.

"You tell the guy who said that ..." He smiled suddenly but softly and let the sentence drift off like a cloud of smoke. "I was in good shape, and he didn't do much for six rounds. Then, in between rounds, I blew my nose and my eye puffed out. The next round he came right out and went after it. Is that carrying me? Was that being kind?"

The kindness actually came before and after the fight.

Known for his pre-fight histrionics and baiting, Ali on that occasion treated Patterson with great respect; afterward with reverence—and a small dose of unintentional condescension. "You fixed all those hypocritical critics," Ali told the defeated warrior. "I'm glad you showed 'em up. You deserve a rematch. Just keep training, Floyd." (Seven years earlier Ali had punished Patterson for 12 rounds for "daring" to call him by the slave name, Cassius Clay.)

The admiration Patterson won for the second battle—admiration from many precincts—he knows he deserved (the fight was stopped before the eighth round began), and it is indelibly written in the catalog of good memories from his years in the ring.

Ali's advice to keep training was superfluous. It seems as though Patterson had spent his days doing little else. He is still in magnificent physical condition, but he is also happily engaged in other activities.

"I'm a boxing commissioner in New York state: I've got five restaurants in Sweden, and I've got 15 to 20 kids like this," he said, pointing around the room. "Those two girls playing ping-pong over there are my daughters. We're together a lot and that's good too. As I said, I'm content."

He then discussed a variety of topics. After talking of his retirement in 1960 ("It took me 12 years to make it stick"), he was asked if Ali would make stick his recent decision to retire.

"I don't think so. He'll let Norton and Forman fight for the vacated championship, then fight Foreman, probably, and be the first man to get the title three times."

Asked what his feelings were after seeing the U.S. Olympic boxing team in action, he replied, "You know what made me proudest? The way those kids talked. Did you hear them speak? They sounded like intelligent gentlemen."

Patterson was interested to find out that the interviewer's wife was Swedish. "Where is she? I'll talk Swedish with her."

He grew more effusive when a young reporter entered the room just as the troupe was preparing to go topside for the bouts. The tardy interviewer noted that he had always admired Patterson, who abruptly asked, "Do *you* think Clay was nice to me?" The fellow was caught off guard and countered, "What did you think of the Ali-Norton fight?"

Patterson sparred with him. "What do *you* think?"

"I think it was a tie, but ties should go to the champion."

"Why is that?" And so on for a playful round or two. The time came to leave. En route to the ring Patterson talked about his farm in New Paltz. Yes, he said, he had spoken at the college there. Once, but never again.

"They're militants. Not me. They're for Black Power; I'm for People Power."

He signed autographs and produced more smiles for youngsters making the requests—particularly the one who caught him a second time. Patterson turned the paper over to show the boy the signed side. The boy shrugged sheepishly; the man signed side two.

He was then introduced to the Swedish wife—in English. "*Vad heter du?*" (What's your name?) he asked perfectly.

"*Jag heter Ulla Anita*," came the reply.

Patterson grinned, his enthusiasm sustained, but his Swedish apparently exhausted. "I spend three months a year there, you know."

During the fights he spent his time watching, sponging and offering advice between rounds. His hands were clasped and his face was glowing as a spindly, hairless-legged adolescent in basketball sneakers shot swift left jabs into the startled face of a more mature, well-turned-out opponent to win the decision. Bout one to Andy Schott of the Hugenot Club.

Patterson is emphatic about his future participation with any of his boys who might become skillful enough to turn pro. "No, I won't manage them or whatever. It wouldn't be fair to them. I don't have the time. I didn't get into this for money. I didn't find them; they found me. It's good this way."

And so Momma Patterson, wherever she is, can rest easy. The wounds have apparently healed, the psychic scars are imperceptible and, in general, things seem to have turned out just fine for her timid boy, Floyd.

Postscript—Floyd Patterson died on May 11, 2006 at the age of 71.

23

No Hugging, Ma'am,
Just the 3 R's

The Rutland Herald, May 4, 1978

It took some time to launch the weekly column for the Herald's 'Southern Vermont Living' section. I somehow had been conned into coaching again, took a women's basketball team to Poland, spent a year involved with the necessary fund-raising activities, taught five Advanced Placement English classes—and continued with some moonlighting so butter would be on the table rather than margarine.

But finally, in April, 1978, I submitted my first weekly column. It was to be called "Miscellany," which could justify, I guess, the assortment of bees buzzing out of my bonnet and typewriter. The first offering was about fishing: the season had begun in a state that held the sport high on its list of direct, meaningful activities. The Battenkill River ran right through my town and Orvis, a prominent fishing equipment company in our town (they've expanded their offerings since then), had international renown and local reverence (jobs!).

But that first column was written from the point of view of an anti-angler. It was nothing against fishing, really. Just a rationalization for my ineptitude with rod and reel. I had never caught a fish. (It was believed by some in my family that I couldn't land one if they stocked the bathtub.)

The second column, the one found below, resulted from a situation within the state that came to my attention. A typical one, I'm sorry to say. About a small town elementary school teacher in Vermont—a young woman doing her damnedest to be a good mentor for her kids. A bunch of mean-spirited parents (I had a mental picture of Mammy Yokums with hairnets and hemorrhoids) joined forces in opposition to this woman and her methodology.

I put in a call to her. She explained what was going on in her classroom in a sensible, non-emotional manner. I liked her. That was all the impetus I required. The rest had already been provided.

Manchester Center—This is a human interest story, for those of you liberal enough to be interested in humans. You should be further warned that it's about a school-teacher. Still with us? You must be a radical.

Here's some background: A couple of weeks ago a UPI news release appearing in this newspaper told of "parent unrest over elementary schoolteacher Pamela Mo-nahan's teaching methods." The article reported that "some parents were unhappy because she allows her students (19 boys and girls in kindergarten through third grade) to sing songs and encourages them to hold hands to show affection for one another." All this in Jay, Vermont.

Strange, indeed. My own recollections provide a vivid picture of limpid-eyed, flaxen-haired Doris, the object of my own third-grade gaze. In those good old days the surest sign of affection was a short and sudden left jab. (Ah, the tenderness of Doris's solar plexus.) And *hugs!* No one dared hug Doris, who, if not stunned by the jab, would launch a devastating bolo punch. Word was that in later years Doris no longer held disdain for affection, real or imagined. She became quite huggable, though in another neighborhood.

But back to the tense present. Parents in Jay also expressed "dissatisfaction" with a new environmental studies course Mrs. Monahan developed and introduced last fall. Nor did they care for the student elections held in class the purpose of which, according to the teacher, is "to demonstrate the democratic process."

Small wonder. Ignorance is bliss at that age. After all, what kind of blissful youth can a primary-age child have with a headful of democratic principles from school and subjection at home? Children should know their place, but do they?

Let us extend some democratic courtesy to the twenty-six-year-old Mrs. Monahan by graciously allowing her to offer attempts to clarify.

"A couple of weeks ago, a parent called me at 11p.m. to tell me a vigilante group was being formed. It was a total surprise to me. I was shocked, having had no trouble prior to this. The chairman of the school board informed me that it was actually three women."

Hadn't Mrs. Monahan "sang all day" with the children? "Ridiculous! We sing two songs to begin each day and have two regularly scheduled music periods during the week. What's really bothering those parents is the unit on democracy. They said I was allowing children to discipline other children. The class president punched someone because he felt he had a leader's right to, but I certainly explained things to him."

A child mature beyond his years: a born leader, surely, who apparently has *not* responded to the hugging program.

Mrs. Monahan mentioned that she could have understood some of the criticism, were her children not performing adequately in the 3 R's. But even standardized test scores, she pointed out, have shown their achievement to be above the national norms in most cases, and near the top in a number of cases.

Part of the enthusiastic young lady's problem is an "open rapport" with her stu-dents. They *like* her, and that may reveal the tragic Jayan flaw: being likeable and being a teacher at the same time. Still, the vast majority of parents seem to accept the flaw and support its possessor.

"I was always willing to make changes, but no critics had anything to say to my face, in order to develop an understanding of what I was doing. My teaching philosophy includes more than just reading, writing and arithmetic. Children must learn how to communicate with each other," offered Mrs. Monahan.

Ay, there's the rub. Such modern theory, she fails to realize, is beyond the ken of many basically competent people, to say nothing of the incompetent.

Last remarks, Mrs. Monahan?

"One of the local old-time Vermonters took this whole thing to the newspapers. He felt I was 'getting sandbagged.' I'm glad to have it out in the open. I do care for quality education. I also know I have a lot to learn."

Correct, Mrs. Monahan. Two things, at least. First, that education shows the wise and hides from the foolish their lack of understanding. Second, that some people are so lost in the thought of what they think they are, they don't see clearly what they ought to be.

For human interest, hang in there, Pammy!

24

A Big Snoot Full of
Very Sour Grapes

The Rutland Herald, June 22, 1978

It was inevitable: lottery tickets were now cascading down the Green Mountains into the hands of the hopers of the world. Of the state, at least. I had written earlier (Article # 8) on the subject of Vermont's being the only state without a lottery. Four years later, Montpelier officials buckled.

Someone once said that a man surprised is half beaten. My better half took the news in stride.

Manchester Center—*Caveat emptor*! Beware of winning the state lottery!! It may be dangerous for your health!!!

That's the warning issued in a new book entitled, *Suddenly Rich.* The admonition comes none-too-soon, with Vermont's new Instant Game having reared its ominous but tempting head two days ago. My cigar box is already full beyond closing with old-fashioned losers. I haven't ever cashed a winning ticket and now, praise be, I discover the beneficent fates have actually been shielding me from the ordeal of being a tragic winner.

"Sudden wealth," announce authors Jerry and Rene Le Blanc, "can pose many problems, and most people aren't prepared for them. It's a vast upheaval in a family. It tests people's images of themselves. It can threaten friendships, put a strain on family relations and even question the importance of what people are doing with their lives."

Let all of us losers join in a moment of silence…

You see, the Le Blancs found that the big hitters complain of being harassed by the public and press (not necessarily in order of disorderliness). The unlucky winners are overcome by letters and telephone calls. The guys at work make jokes. The old neighborhood just isn't the same anymore—and the new ones, with their high-class inhabitants, aren't particularly comfy, if you know what I mean. Mr. and Mrs.

Unlucky become nervous and suspicious. They may live on the move, or buy guns. Strangers loiter; burglaries are common.—"There is a good deal to fear."

Stop giggling, losers. Many sad stories are recounted in *Suddenly Rich*. One lottery-mad millionaire says: "The neighbors and people down the street who used to talk to us got very quiet when we'd go by. They seemed to feel that we were rich."

Easy for you to scratch your head, losers; you're probably poor and incapable of empathy. But try to relate to one poor rich fellow who, in the book, wishes that he knew then what he knows now. *That* even a loser can understand. And so it goes. Quite a sobering story does the volume tell. And the Vermont experience might very well be included in this anthology of misery. There are signs.

Since its Valentine's Day inception, our own state lottery has produced two $100,000 prize-winners: $10,000 a year for ten years, each receives. One innocent resides part-time in the heart of Rutland, the other in the extremity of Graniteville. Both shall remain nameless, of course. The Rutland chap, a man of about thirty, has taken the predictable precaution of having his telephone number unlisted. He was not pursued further by this writer, lest he had purchased a weapon to insure sustained privacy.

When the gentleman in Graniteville was recently rung up, a teenage voice on the other end, avowing to the same surname as the lottery winner, assured the anonymous caller that though the 'winner' had not yet returned from work (a positive indication), he would be home shortly and would be "happy to talk to anybody." Despite the youthful optimism, ensuing rings went unanswered through the night. One can imagine the travail at the other end of the wire.

Unaware of such circumstances, thousands of hopeful and avaricious Vermonters continue to swell their hearts and the treasury's pockets.

"Yes, the Vermont Lottery is doing very well," boasts administrative manager, Ralph Peters, an articulate spokesman whose position allows him immunity from the strain of greed. "No, I can't buy tickets. We have to keep the system above reproach, you know." Little does he realize his position of advantage, though no actual credit should be given to him for willful abstinence.

By the end of this month, a total of $300,000 will have been funneled into the state's general fund by the lottery. This week's new game (instant winners of up to $5,000) promises to add to the public coffers and to private grief.

In Danby, an optimistic enthusiast, Mrs. Frieda Eaves, revealed some small success: an assortment of winnings—$20 and $5 varieties—adding up to $60 in profit. Her purchasing system has been a popular one, a weekly investment of $5—ten tickets in a string which assures one ticket of being numerically eligible for the big drawing.

When advised of the undesirable effects of winning big, Mrs. Eaves seemed rightfully concerned and rapidly converted. She took the message as a welcome warning. "Might as well quit," she reasoned, just under her breath. "I haven't won anything the last two weeks anyhow." The convert's means need not be important to a missionary's end.

A Rutland High School senior had been adhering to the same technique: weekly investments of $5. His winnings were close to $100. The lottery provided a $1,000 graduation ticket recently. A harbinger of doom, I assume. He will soon be contacted.

There is the happier case of Mrs. Marion Zoufaly of Manchester, who thought she had scaled new personal heights by winning $1 in a supermarket game. She turned her profits into a neophyte's parlay: two lottery tickets during the game's first week. One brought back $1,000 for the lady. It also brought a letter of congratulations from the state, including a not-too-subtle reminder that she owed them a piece of the action.

But that was all the action Mrs. Z., a visionary, cared for. She did not play the lottery again, though for the sake of truth, it must be mentioned that since that lottery win, she has also won a service organization's door prize and a loaf of bread (albeit over-baked) in an elementary school raffle drawing. The evil fates are obviously conspiring, but Mrs. Z., having withstood the lottery's temptation, prevails.

So should it be for anyone who reads these words or those of Jerry and Rene Le Blanc. And if those words are not enough, one question remains: What should a proud and savvy Vermonter want from a game of questionable chance initially instituted by the state of New Hampshire?

"Just a few big ones," answers my wife, whose six-digit dream for today's drawing is 4-02-313.

Don't call us if it's a winner.

25

A Barrel Full
of Uneeda Philosophy

The Rutland Herald, August 3, 1978

One of the many unpleasant and useless experiences I had with doctors as a bed-ridden asthmatic child brought me to an allergist who punctured my arm with thousands of needle points and put me on an eating program that would have had Gandhi asking for seconds.

It was awful. No meat, no dairy products. No sense. I lost weight and was weakened to the point of being taken to a train at Grand Central Station in a wheel chair to see a 'quack' doctor in Mississippi, who started me on the road to resistance. (Of other doctors and my bullying pathology.)

A few years before taking that trip, I had lobbied my mother to have some mercy at breakfast, at least. The usual fare had been a raw egg, barely strained, put into a glass of evaporated milk. (Repulsive.) This, the allergist said, was certainly allowable. (Jerk.) My appeal was based on observation of my father relishing Uneeda Biscuits, lightly buttered and washed down by his morning coffee. I wanted that fare. It took persistence, and I knew my mother was not a good fighter, so I kept at her. Finally, I won.

Did I ever! I loved it. I looked forward to breakfast. The taste buds of my memory still enjoy the experience.

In 1978, almost accidentally, I found myself looking into the background of the biscuit that ultimately banished raw egg-in-you-know-what.

Manchester Center & Fair Lawn, New Jersey—"They hain't no more, least not as been meant to be." The succinct response came from a weathered but formidable Vermont gentleman.

He had been asked about the chances of finding a cracker barrel in any of the vicinity's country stores. An oak of a man, his words hung like lifeless boughs of time. "Fact of the matter," he went on, "hain't even a real country store t'speak of—least not as been meant to be." The lament was clothed in a smile. Scantily clothed.

Indeed, the cracker barrel "hain't no more." The origin of its obsolescence can be traced back to the year 1899, when its utility—as first meant to be—was usurped. Following came many years of retirement as the cynosure in lively country stores where townsmen foregathered to philosophize, to tell tales, to play checkers. Now, only in American Yankee lore does the cracker barrel live on.

But still quintessentially in evidence are the soda-cracker contents of those early wooden barrels.

Known as Uneeda Biscuit since 1899 (recognize that date?), these delicate survivors indicate that perhaps eternity does love some productions of time.

I've come to find out that revelations usually leap from casuality. That cracker-barrel inquiry led to a personal re-acquaintance with Uneeda Biscuits, the very morsels I first washed over and down with delectable morning coffee as a boy in my ninth year—and daily thereafter, until my departure from the hearth to college. There were still the occasional prerequisites on the menu materfamilias: raw eggs in evaporated milk. But then came the joyous compensation. Dessert, so to say. The very nourishment I quirkily craved during the formative years. (Wonder Bread be damned.) And the very product which hastened the cracker barrel's formal retirement.

It was actually the crackers' packaging that rolled the barrel out of its job. The innovative package allowed Uneedas to retain their freshness until eaten, owing to a waxed-paper-lined carton. Previously, tin cans had been the exclusive protective food packages.

The prohibitive cost of the cans precluded their use for preserving small quantities of crackers to be sold as a popular price. (Following Uneeda's lead, many food products leaped from bulk barrels and boxes into handy and practical packages: butter, cheese, flour, bread, sugar, tea, coffee and so on.)

In 1898, one Adolphus Green, a Chicago lawyer, brought three cracker-baking companies into a consolidation called the National Biscuit Company. Shortly thereafter, Mr. Green decided to abandon his law practice to devote his mental energies and physical diligence to crackers. At the time, crackers were marketed in large communal barrels, but Green began to speak inspirationally of small-unit packaging and a five-cent selling price.

Each small carton, he theorized, would hold "no greater quantity than would practically always be consumed while in a palatable condition," packed in a way that "no contamination from moisture, dust, germs, odors, human or animal contacts" might adversely affect the crackers. He had trumpeted a general call for *the* proper package, and, as Victor Hugo had written, "No army can withstand the strength of an idea whose time has come."

Success for Uneeda Biscuit was immediate and impressive. At the turn of the century, in the product's second year, 10,000 packages (at a nickel per) were sold each month.

Grocers, skeptical when Uneedas were introduced (and worried that a 20 percent profit on the crackers was too thin), began to queue up their wagons at the New York City bakery, impatient for deliveries by the company. The retailers had learned their lesson the easy way—with a quick turnover which brought in more profits than the cheaper barrel crackers with their breakage, spoilage and considerably smaller sales volume.

Eighty years later—today—Uneeda Biscuit hangs in a pendulous state, clinging to a thread called 'loyalty.' The tenacity of the grip may be of little ultimate consequence, for the only corporate pendulum that swings in perpetuity is called 'profit.' 'Sales' more informally. Of Nabisco's thirteen plants across the country, only one continues to make Uneeda Biscuit—on a limited scale, at that.

At the Fair Lawn, N.J., bakery, Uneedas are produced once a week. Usually. In 1958, when the plant began its operation, Uneedas were baked four days a week. Salted and unsalted. Now, alas, only unsalted are made, though this fact in itself does not seem significant to at least one connoisseur. (Salted were superfluous.) More significantly, production is currently under 800,000 packages per month and waning. But devotion to the product is constant enough.

In Fair Lawn, two 'old-timers' maintain an affinity with their company's former cracker-darling. (Oreo and Ritz are executive pets these days.) Both men moved from the New York bakery to help open the Jersey plant. Both are now thirty-plus-year men. Bakery supervisor Roy Boutin has seen many changes in the cookie-and-cracker world, but Uneeda ingredients, he reports with obvious pride, "have remained the same as always."

Packaging is Leo Uscinski's domain. Mr. Uscinski sounds more the philosopher than the practitioner. "The difference in packaging is that now there is an end-opening box." It is a curt dismissal of physical matters. His concern abruptly turns to Uneeda's diminishing role in contemporary life. Once stocked in just about every grocery store in the country, Uneeda Biscuit now has a market limited to "the East," says Mr. O. sadly.

"New England, really," he qualifies. "There are so many other soda crackers now. Premium Saltines are our best seller. Have you ever seen a kid eating Uneedas lately?" The question, a rhetorical one, is voiced in a premonitory tone.

"I think we keep baking them because it was the first packaged cracker." He brightens. "Old men who've lost their dentures are the only ones who eat 'em now. They dip Uneedas in warm milk." He laughs heartily, then finds his more serious self and discourses to a conclusion. A terse summation: the present contains nothing but the past. What is found in the effect was already in the cause.

Cracker barrel philosophy actuel. Too bad that old, oaken Vermont gentleman wasn't there to share his views—dunk a few soda crackers, perhaps.

Despite forebodings, the Big Biscuit hangs on.

And for the time being, knowing more about Uneedas than need be known, I once again breakfast on these crumbling delights, accompanied by more than a few evocative memories.

Postscript—Nabisco stopped producing Uneedas in January, 2009. They still make Animal Crackers, but ...

26

Turning Back to One
Who Made a Mark

The Rutland Herald, August 10, 1978

By 1978 I had *been teaching for twenty-one years. At the end of the school year, for no reason known to me, I received an inordinate number of thoughtful and kind thank-you notes and letters from my high school students. Yet I was disturbed.*

One of my own high school English teachers had had a great influence on me—and I had never offered the thanks due him. I called the DeWitt Clinton High School alumni office and hoped my inquiry would be answered in the way I wanted it—needed it—to be. The guy was still alive and living on Pelham Parkway, I was told. (I wrote about this in my anecdotal memoir.) The call went splendidly. He remembered me (he would) and we gabbed at length. He enjoyed my writings in the Times, *he said, and then went ranting, as in the old days, about corrupt and ignorant politicians. Still very much alive.*

One down, one more to go, I thought after having hung up the phone. Another 25-years-overdue thank you had to be made. This one, I decided, I would make in person. And the article below was written after that obligation was met.

In the context of the piece, I avoid presenting the specific personal act this man made—one that certainly influenced my life. This I knew in 1978. But in 2011, I understand that it was a dramatic *influence, given all that happened to me since the article was written. The career/life changes since '78 could not have been possible without this man's influence.*

I'll try to be brief. I went to Brockport State Teachers College, not because I wanted to teach, but because it was a small state school that my family could afford and one small enough that I might be able to play on an inter-collegiate varsity team.

Another agenda of mine: I enrolled as a physical education major, using Teddy Roosevelt, another asthmatic, as a model for 'fightin' the damn pathology.' I wasn't a rough-rider exactly, but those gymnastic horses would have to do.

I never had the chance to mount one. I was drummed out of the program within two weeks, doomed by a course called "Rhythms and Dance" (the male students referred to it as *"Brownies and Fairies"). It required too much constant exertion for me. The instructor, a woman very serious about her course offering and the students' obligations to it, tried to let me down easy. "You can transfer to General Ed., Harvey." Which I did.*

The school physician, aware of my asthma (plenty of meds had already been dispensed as per my requests) and now informed of my being dropped from the physical education program, told me I was not to participate in soccer any longer. They couldn't take the chance. Whatever that meant.

But I went to practice. The coach said nothing. I spent at least ten days looking over my shoulder, avoiding the doctor, wondering what was going on—and practicing every day.

Then the shoe dropped—softly. As I crossed the parking lot after having come out of the school building, a car pulled up next to me. It was Dr. Sansoucie. He rolled down his window and said, "How's soccer going, Harvey?" I was flummoxed, caught off guard. I stammered, not wanting to incriminate myself—reveal my insubordination. I was fearing the worst. But he abruptly rolled up the car window and drove off.

What had happened? The only explanation I have ever been able to come up with is that the coach—who I know watched me carefully (and appreciated what I was trying to do for myself—to say nothing of my inclination to be a team player), explained to the doctor how much this meant to me—and that to take soccer away from me would _____. (Fill in the blank.)

I became close with the doctor. I babysat his young son. He came to games. Not a word was ever spoken about his original mandate or the tricky business of "How's soccer going …?" And so, of course, I never thanked him. Until 1978, 25 years after those happenstances.

Quite a long intro to this piece—and still more could be said about how competing in an elite soccer program prepared me for a career in sport psychology. But enough.

Brockport, N.Y.—In its simplest sense this is a family vacation. The children are going somewhere. The parents are going anywhere to get away from somewhere. In a physical sense, it may be better to be in southern Vermont in summertime than to be out of it. The heat and humidity here defy metaphor.

No environment, however, can compete with primeval expanses: places and times which inhibit or prohibit telephone calls, newspapers, visitors and routine; places and time which usher in anonymity, regenerate the spirit and reaffirm our own individual existence. An offering of change is made to the psyche, and it is gratefully accepted.

Brockport—and there is such a place—is not actually included in the vacation itinerary. It is one stop on a debtor's pilgrimage, recently begun so as to fill the debtor's body by expanding the soul.

The debt is too long overdue, although the payment itself is meager. All that need be given is a "Thank you." The gratitude has been too long sealed in silence. The action must now stand up to the professed faith.

Readers will be spared details of the debt, since these details are too personal to satisfy the wise and not personal enough to satisfy the foolish. The focus lies beyond all this, and now is as good a time as any to move in that direction.

In each of our lives there are crucial junctures, and very often—by choice or chance—we approach them in loneliness that envelopes a secret society of one. One who struggles through a personal process of decision-making, self-assessment or general problem-solving.

These pivotal points are more numerous during the earlier years—young adulthood. At this stage, a few fortunates stumble through a solitary tunnel of darkness toward the light they eventually discover at the other end. The more fortunate have their way lighted. In many cases, the torch is held by people who come into their lives at the right time, at the right place. The passage is made safely, or wisely or comfortably, due in great measure, to the light of those torch-holders, with whom contact may be quickly lost. They may not have even been aware of the intensity of the glow they provided. And, for that matter, neither may the solitary tunnel-traveler.

Unless he remembers to turn back.

Brockport is one in the recently begun series of turnings back, in this case to student days at the State University of New York.

I check the town's local telephone directory and find the name I seek: Carl Sansoucie, M.D. A call is placed, and a recorded voice soothes the feelings of discomfort which accompany unpreparedness. I do not know what to say to the nurse-secretary. A part of my day is devoted to the deficiency.

The next morning, after initial telephone contact, I announce myself at the doctor's office. He has an unexpected delivery at the hospital, a Caesarean section, and will arrive at the office at 11:30 or so. I chat with the nurse, who now knows my purpose without the particulars. I then depart.

At 11:30 I return and am escorted to a waiting room. The kindly nurse offers coffee. Accepted.

Moments later Dr. Carl Sansoucie enters. Greetings. Of course, he knows why I am here, but no, he does not realize that a singular act of his had such a great impact on his visitor's life.

"I owe you," I hear myself say. Then talking in a succession of small squeaks, I reconstruct past events and define a pivotal point—the one at which he stood. The nature of the debt is explained to a doctor whose instrument was not medical, but whose beam of light came from knowing there are cures which required no less than his respect for what was unknown to him. A doctor who sensed that someone who does not go through the inferno of his own passions can never overcome them, or much else.

"And finally," I say in an effort to prevent descent to maudlin sentimentality, "Thank you."

I want to add someone else's words: "Only the wounded physician heals." But I am silent in respect for the 25 years which have made us strangers to each other.

And he is a busy man. Still, he talks for a time on some subjects of mutual familiarity. Then he is gone.

It's over. The gesture has been made to another of the precious few people left behind who shared a secret without a realization, who made a mark without recognizing its indelibility, who watched the wearer disappear, never expecting a reappearance.

"It's nice to know I did *something* right," Carl Sansoucie had said minutes before, in an awkward confluence of humility, pride and appreciation.

Although the visit, to the visitor, is only a proper deed in an improper world, the good doctor's countenance suggested it may have become an eternal one, at that. But such possibility is irrelevant.

Or is it?

Tomorrow to Toronto and to a family vacation in the simplest sense.

Can it be this hot in Vermont?

27

Dear Ms. Jane Pauley

The Rutland Herald, May 3, 1979

I returned to employing the 'letter format' again with this piece. I again adopted the persona of a seemingly innocent, self-effacing letter-writer who knows more than he lets on. I only wish I could become one of these prototypical Vermonters. Anyhow, I tried to talk the talk, albeit in print.

All the circumstances leading to the piece are spelled out within its context, so the reader can be spared a lengthy introduction, such as the one accompanying the previous article.

One thing I will say: Many years later—many—I saw Jane Pauley again on television. I heard her, more importantly—and she sounded mature, sensible and—dare I say it?—likeable. OK, I'll say it.

I wonder if my letter—dare I say this?—helped start her on the way to personal and professional growth. I'll not say it.

Today Show
NBC
New York, N.Y.
May 3, 1979

Dear Ms. Pauley,

Well, today Spring is proving it can handle its annual conflict with Winter here in Vermont. The sun looks pretty confident, the crocuses are believing in themselves too, and the phoebes are acting serious about their renovation job right outside my window. The struggle is over, I think, although I haven't witnessed much of it this year.

My own struggles have kept me pretty much indoors lately. Right now—today— I'm struggling with chicken pox. The thing is, Ms. Pauley, I'm 43 years old and look "very gross," according to my children. So don't worry, this letter isn't asking for a dinner date or anything such.

The letter's probably being written out of boredom. You might think that after reading it. But actually, I'm writing to cheer you up, though you are not a shut-in, as I am at the moment. What happened, Ms. Pauley, was that in an effort to forget myself, I found you. I turned on the television set yesterday morning. I rarely do that at any hour. But there you were on a show called *Today*. I'd never heard of you. My daughter (she's got chicken pox, too) says you replaced Barbara Walters, and that you "look like her and talk like her." Is that good? I have never heard of her either. The last ladies I ever heard of on TV are Arlene Francis, Faye Emerson and Dagmar. Do you work with any of them? If so, please send them my best wishes; they're some entertainers!

Anyhow, back to cheering you up, Ms. Pauley. I saw your interview with Margaret Trudeau, "the estranged wife" of Canada's prime minister, and I saw how you got egg on your face in front of hundreds of viewers. (My daughter says millions, but you know how teenagers exaggerate.) You sure didn't have a grip on matters, and I'm sure you felt the egg right there, though you—and your colleagues—didn't admit it. You tried to make Mrs. Trudeau look worse than my daughter says she looks without getting any help. You did this to get the attention away from the egg, of course, but it was sort of graceless for a TV lady. But who can blame you? In front of all those viewers. Goodness, who knows what I would have done? I just thought about how I'd like to have your audience looking at me with all these chicken pox!

Interviewing people is a tough business. Plenty of stupid questions—such as a few you asked—have been asked by thousands of interviewers. I've asked my share. But usually, praise be, the answers are just as foolish. Sometimes more so. Too bad for you, Ms. Pauley, that Mrs. Trudeau saw right away the childishness and shallowness of your harping on the name of her unidentified (in her book) Southern gentleman. Why did you dally with that? You look like a high type, Ms. Pauley. Not as high as Margaret Truman, I said to my daughter. (She said Margaret Truman plays "Hollywood Squares," but I don't understand teenage slang.) But a high type, I thought. Anyhow, you sure didn't raise yourself with that irrelevant prying, missing the point about the shabby ways of the press, missing an allusion to the business of defining one's reality. You could have picked up on that. Instead, I think, you did become the very model of what Mrs. Trudeau said was deplorable—that was the word—about so many people in the media.

Well, I saw you weren't any too happy when Mrs. T. took you to task. You gave it a country try at recovery though, telling her she was a contradiction which, of course, she is. But after all, Ms. Pauley, we're all contradictions—trying to grow a staple crop in a field of conflicting impulses.

I don't know much about Mrs. Trudeau—only what my daughter tells me—but you made me like her a bit, so cheer up, you did something real good. Now, I know you're a busy person, but I just want to mention that I saw a commercial message during your program, one about a product that can make things grow fast and furious, even in sand, though I don't believe *that*. It sort of reminded me of what a farmer here once told me after he read an article about himself in a magazine. "Mistakes," he said to me. "Mistakes is the hardiest plants. They grow in every soil." *That* I believe. Take it for what it's worth, Ms. Pauley.

So here I am, banging out this good cheer to you on my typewriter, watching myself turn into Scabman. Luckily, you'll never have to see me. I'll probably never see you again, for that matter. I'm hoping to be better real soon. I hope you are too, Ms. Pauley.

Best wishes,
H.A. Dorfman

28

A 19-Year-Old Metamorphosis

The Rutland Herald, May 17, 1979

Some of the great rewards that came from writing these columns were letters I received with all manner of comments, all very interesting, most very appreciative and kind, some quite enlightening.

I will ask forgiveness for my being somewhat immodest by including a portion from one such a letter. It was written by the wife of the Assistant Headmaster at the school where I was a faculty member. I use it as the Postscript. The letter—and the article, of course—relate to a young man I had as a student for six years—in junior and senior high school. Many of my students had similar difficulties. This fellow probably had more than the others.

David and I had a good relationship: I worked patiently with him on his reading and social skills; he worked patiently with me on fixing my lawn mower or chain saw or car motor. Well, to tell the truth, he worked patiently as I watched helplessly but appreciatively.

Manchester—The daily announcements for students at Burr & Burton Seminary on May 9 included the following notation:

"Mr. David Brooks, a former student at BBS and presently in the U.S. Army, will be here today during G-Block to talk with students about the various opportunities and careers the Army provides. If you are interested in talking with Mr. Brooks and learning more about the U.S. Army, come to the Guidance Office."

Mr. David Brooks! MISTER David Brooks!!

David Brooks is a 19-year-old metamorphosis. He is big, red-headed, clean-shaven, neatly attired, erect, confident, responsible, clear-thinking and proud.

He's always been big and red-headed. All the rest are new to him. David enlisted in the Army last August and reported for duty Nov. 1. The transformation can be traced to that date.

David Brooks looks back: "I didn't like school from the time I started as a kid, and I guess I showed it. I couldn't do much. My reading was terrible. I couldn't write. I'd see other kids' papers and compare them to mine. I saw how bad mine were. A teacher would say something supposed to make me feel good, I guess: a compliment."

He waves his hand in a gesture of disdain. "I knew it was bull."

David was and is a bright young person. As is the case with many school children, his mental acuity was veiled by a complexity of skill deficiencies, immaturity, insecurity, lack of motivation and resultant behavioral difficulties.

"I hated it. I couldn't learn to read. If I knew there was an assignment to read aloud next day, I'd be absent. If kids were reading in order, going around the room, I'd figure when my turn would come and get out of that room somehow.

"By the seventh and eighth grade I'd stay home and hide behind the hill. When I went, I didn't do anything. I wasn't able to do much, and no one thought I ever would, I guess."

He couldn't hide very effectively; he was over six feet in height by then. His records suggested dyslexia, motor skill weaknesses, sight difficulties and other characteristic problems attributed to poor learners. He was working with record players, tapes, slides and all sorts of manipulatives. The printed word was a nemesis not to be confronted.

David became the number one project in the Burr & Burton reading program when he arrived there. He spent his entire high school career in the program and by graduation time last June had scored above the 11th grade on a number of standardized reading materials. Printed materials.

But another problem had developed during this time. David's social pattern had the design for trouble. Plenty of it. All sorts. Here was this big, quiet, good—yes, good—kid, who always seemed to be doing something wrong—by design or destiny. He was accused of more than was deserved. When the accusations were deserved, David's eyes were all interrogators need deal with.

He clowned; he cavorted: a motorcycle ride up the front walk of the school—across the soggy athletic field. Innocent escapades in abundance; minor accidents occasionally; some form of trouble continuously. Malicious? No. Likable? Yes? Irritating? Of course. Worrisome? Exceedingly.

"Football helped me a lot," he says quietly after the other memories recede. Big and strong, he appeared a good prospect as a tackle. "I was voted L.V.P.," he sighs. "Least valuable player. It still helped to be out there."

Football was an asparagus seed. Three years to wait for the real thing. "After graduation, I guess I knew it would be best for me to leave Manchester. A few people even told me that."

And he left in November. Not only to shuck a local label, but, insightfully, to escape prospects in Manchester which were dim and, perhaps, dangerous.

Fort McClellan, Alabama, Nov. 1, 1978.

THE date.

Says Private Brooks: "I got off the bus with a bunch of other guys and we were all lined up. My shirt button was open, and the Army guy tells me to button it up. I've got a big smile on my face: I think he's kidding. He wasn't.

"For the first two weeks I did the opposite of everything I was told. There were so many ridiculous orders. I screwed so many things up, and I didn't care about anything."

Army sergeants can hardly be credited for Aristotelian justice when they "give to every man his own." But what they gave David Brooks was finally enough to convince him he had determined adversaries.

"I got tired fighting them."

He had constructed a wall around his loneliness; in his weary isolation he decided to try building bridges instead.

"I started to hear what I was being told, and I obeyed. All of a sudden they were saying, 'Nice bed, Brooks.' Then, 'Your boots are looking good, Brooks.'"

David had recognized the undeserved praise he'd been given in school and had considered it to be unintentional satire. The small gestures commending his bed and boots he was ready to consider as recompense for things truly done. He discovered pride. A creative pride.

"Yes, that's what did it. I really started to feel good about things, proud of myself. What the Army really did, I figured, was to tear everybody right down. We were all nobodies, all the same. We all started even."

This, David Brooks figured out, was an opportunity to discover a new persona. Though the discovery still left him two weeks behind, he closed the gap rapidly.

"You're told to do 40 physical tasks in 10 minutes. You know you can't do it, but you try it so they won't bug you. After a while, you're doing it out of pride, and after another while you're doing more than you ever thought you could."

A smile of recollection crosses his face.

"A couple of us stayed at camp over Christmas. Everyone else shipped out. We looked at the bunk floor one night and it wasn't right. We worked eight hours washing, waxing, buffing and stripping it when it still wasn't right. When we finished, we looked at it and each other and couldn't believe it. 'Did I do that?' I said to myself—and I started to strip my uniform off. I thought for a few seconds I was crazy. It was only pride."

David finished basic training in Fort Eustace, Virginia, and was then assigned to duty as a recruiter. For 30 days he worked out of the Bennington Recruiting Station. And last week he was at his old high school. He showed slides, talked, answered questions and looked like a general to younger students (and a few of his former teachers) who remembered the wild kid who used to be "Brooksie."

What did he say in his sales pitch?

"I showed the same slides and pictures I looked at last year. But I told them they're not seeing it at all. You only see what's supposed to be the good stuff. The bad stuff isn't in the pictures. But that's the stuff that makes you into something. I tell them that."

David moved on to Fort Bless, Texas, last Saturday. (His mother probably celebrated her happiest—proudest?—Mother's Day in years, despite the departure of her boy the day before.) In Texas, he will spend a year training as a Scout helicopter repairman. He intends to be an auto mechanic when his enlistment time is up. His father, who was a talented musician, had a reputation in Manchester as the most astute mechanic for the most sophisticated engines. He died five years ago.

"Aviation mechanics is the hardest to do. That's why I chose it. Then I'll study auto mechanics," David explains. "I want to come home and start up my father's garage again."

It is not a physical building David wishes to resurrect but something which, though more abstract, is more substantial.

"I loved him," says the son. "I still do."

Thomas Wolfe said that you can't go home again. MISTER David Brooks thinks he can.

Postscript—Note from Nancy Otis—"… and today, the one on David Brooks 'took the cake.' Not only did I have a tear in the eye, the lump in my throat, etc.—but also a measure of guilt for not having had more faith in the lad, especially having known his parents …In fact, Don said, as he passed me the Herald. *'Be sure and read Harvey today.' Then he added, 'It's on David Brooks.'*

I said, 'David Brooks, the delinquent?' Don knows how many times I had expressed myself thus, especially when Dave was employed by the Pro Shop at (the golf course). Guess my lack of perception is why I'm not a teacher, but I'm disappointed in myself anyway. Let this be a lesson to me. A beautiful piece of writing—and understanding. Thank you!
Sincerely,
Nancy

29

Their Night at the Races

The Rutland Herald, May 31, 1979

Lorraine and I began our teaching careers in 1957. Same school. Same grade level (5th). Some differences, of course. She was a Queens County girl; I was a Bronx boy. She was married; I was joyfully single.

The following year, Anita showed up to teach 3rd grade. Months into the school year, we began dating. No one in the school knew about it. Except Lorraine. That's the way Anita and I wanted it. No gossip; no questions from other faculty members. My trust in Lorraine was well deserved.

She and her husband, Jerry (not a teacher), and Anita and I double-dated a few times. Then we started hanging out on a more regular basis on weekends and vacations. A friendship ensued. That was more than 50 years ago. The friendship endures.

Amazingly, Lorraine and Jerry still live in the same house they were in when we first met, whereas Anita and I have resided at eight different addresses in four different states over the years. Our children (Allison, their daughter, and Melissa and Dan, our two) have happy memories of antics they witnessed and participated in during get-togethers at these various venues. As Emerson suggested, the blessing of having an old friend is that you can "afford to be stupid" with him—or her.

All that as it is, the inclusion of this piece is based on my belief that such a relationship merits acknowledgement. Though the reporting of a night at a dog track doesn't embrace it in its entirety, it does tickle my fancy, and it provides a glimpse of a woman who need not be tortured in order to elicit her opinions.

Manchester Center—She and he were Memorial Day weekend guests again. On Saturday morning I told her of my plans. She said that one thing she never wanted to do was go to the dog races. I told her friendship is one mind in two bodies. Besides I had to go.

On the way to Pownal she was still adamant. Her father had worked as a concessionaire at New York horse racing tracks. She had come up to Saratoga to see the great Kelso run his last race on an oppressively hot day 14 summers ago. Persistence is one of her great and necessary virtues.

She said that if horse racing is the sport of kings, dog racing must be the folly of jesters. As her inclinations, so her opinions. She had wanted to see Woody Allen's *Manhattan* in Rutland this night. The lines in New York had been impossible, the wait longer than the movie itself, she said.

We sped south on Route 7. I spoke calmly and generally. She said she might have to move up front. The road was getting her car-sick. She said this was entirely insane. I told her sanity is a matter of degree. Falling drops trying to wear down stone.

She said they ought to race poodles and dachshunds and so on. That might make it interesting. He laughed. They have their own 16-year-old blind dog. It has no particular breed or distinguishing achievements aside from its longevity. Its name is Cutie. I told her Cutie might surprise her and turn up in one of the races. Contemptible contempt, she said. He laughed.

She asked how many races were on the night's agenda. I told her 15 on the track's agenda. She said she could tolerate five. I told her we would be in the midst of our clubhouse dinner that short time. She said she couldn't chance looking at a menu at a dog track. She said the whole thing was barbaric.

I told her that dogs had raised their status in civilization since their days of bear baiting and ratting. She said man is the only animal that blushes—or has cause to. Mark Twain, I told her.

We were all settled in our dining-table seats. One seafood platter; one club sandwich; one fruit salad plate. She had ordered pork. She said the green beans were terrible.

We looked over the racing program then made our bets for the first race. The eight dogs were marched past the clubhouse and grandstand by eight teenage girls to the accompaniment of a recording of "Anchors Aweigh." She said the music was symbolically absurd. He stopped tapping his foot.

She said the betting system was just as bad: quinellas, trifectas, tri-wheeling and tri-boxing. The tote board showed no one played it straight. Gimmicks! Not for sporting gamblers or form followers; for obsessive get-rich-quickers. Desperate, she said.

They're not horse players here. They smoke as obsessively as they bet. The men wear their shirts out of their pants, have slick hair and look constipated. The women have their hair wired, walk as if their ankles are tied together and smile—if that's what they're doing—with their lips closed. She said all this.

The first race took under 33 seconds to run; the longest race took just under 40. Not much time to build an excitement, she said—if you're inclined.

She asked later who I had in the eighth race. I told her York Scott, number six. She tilted her head toward me slightly and said Tony's Joanie. Going into the first turn,

York Scott challenged for the lead—then went tumbling sideways out of the pack. Over and over went York Scott. Again she tilted her head slightly.

Tony's Joanie won the race. She looked into her coffee cup and said nothing.

It was 11 o'clock. I told her we'd probably had enough. She said one more race. Cutie Mo was running in the 12th. So it was! Here was Cutie after all, at 50-1. Appropriate odds for a blind dog, I told her. She bet it to show, which it did. She had a fistful of third place tickets. We waited, laughing, while she cashed in. Then we left.

Out of the darkness of the car, she said it had been fun. I told her I had known. They laughed.

I am very fond of her.

30

Dealing with Skeptics, the Little League, Coaches and Mothers

The Rutland Herald, June 7, 1979

As a kid who grew up on the sandlots, light years before the advent of Little League, I must confess to a bias against the very idea of the organization. I advocate play by youngsters that adults have nothing to do with. Without coaches and parents intervening—supervening!

Do I suggest a return to what codgers call 'the good old days'? No, I'm smarter than that. Still, I have my memories: going out of the apartment house I lived in on weekend mornings—glove and bat in hand and parental order in mind: "Be home in time for dinner."

So it was with those fond recollections in mind that I stuck my fingers into my typewriter keyboard and my tongue into my cheek. This piece is the result.

Manchester—Did you know that New England's Joey Jay (Middletown, Connecticut) was the first Little Leaguer ever to become a major league baseball player? I know! (Milwaukee Braves, 1953-1956; Cincinnati Reds, 1961-1966; Atlanta Braves, 1968.)

I also know that it is unpolished to be self-laudatory, but it is nevertheless important to establish my credibility as a Little League historian. I go way back with the Little League, you see, as an observer and a self-appointed consultant. And I have acted as a mediator, breaking up fights between and among spectator-parents: father vs. father; mother vs. mother; father vs. mother; mother vs. father; inter- and intra-family melees and tag team matches.

When a girl was not permitted to participate in Little League play years back, because local rules mandated that all players had to wear protective cups, and her parents and physician thought it ridiculous in her case, I designed a lovely cup-necklace, fashioned it and sent it to the family. It allowed the youngster to be both decorated and dignified and, at the same time, to be in compliance with the rule.

When Little League officials banned Taiwan from competition, and many accused these officials of sour grapes because the Orientals had won the championship too often, I was sympathetic, understanding and—I thought—constructive. I knew the actual reason for the Taiwan expulsion was the sad fact that these foreigners did not provide the optimum social experience for our American youngsters, an experience which the Little League Charter recognizes as being almost as important as winning. Few people realize it was my suggestion that these officials emphasize their point by throwing out all New Jersey teams as well, since New Jerseyites presented the same problem as Taiwanese. I did not, contrary to accusations by my detractors, seriously advocate the admittance of a team from Borneo as a token replacement for Taiwan. As a matter of historical fact, Borneo had voted a year earlier against having Little Leagues in their country for some reason or another.

I have lost, so to speak, my own flesh and blood in Little League combat, so I am emotionally, as well as historically, involved. My tiny nephew's right elbow joint was destroyed from throwing a wicked and winning screwball when he was eight. He won the league's Most Valuable Player Award, though he was later humiliated by a 4-F classification during the Vietnam War. However, it had been a proud and poignant moment years before, when his old and loving grandfather came up at the awards banquet to help the maimed boy carry his trophy back to their table.

And over the years I have seen significant progress in all Little League environments. For example, spectators are no longer permitted to bring bullhorns with them into the stands. (Unfortunately—though Darwin would appreciate the irony—evolution has been responsible for the development of greater lung and vocal cord capabilities since the advent of Little League competition. The bullhorn has become unnecessary, in addition to being unlawful.) Further, spectators may now scream only at their own children and at opposing coaches. Weapons must be left in parked cars, and drinking on the premises is not tolerated, with the understandable exception being the umpires.

On next year's docket are considerations to administer basic competency tests to prospective coaches (not retroactive) and to disallow crying (by players only, during a trial period), even after losses of big games.

Recent sociological studies have given hints that player anxiety has decreased over the years. It is outrageous that one so-called social scientist claimed "The kids just don't give a damn anymore."

Very emphatically, one Robin Dame does give a damn. Robin Dame is a 9-year-old girl who, according to a front page report last week in this very newspaper, had been dropped from the Hartford Little League. There was mention in the report of an ensuing court battle, should the alleged ban continue.

Continue? All this must have been a mistake! Every coach had to have watched "The Bad News Bears" as a training film. And this is the age of enlightenment, insofar as treatment of females is concerned. Few men any longer believe, as James Thurber suggested, that a woman's place is in the wrong.

So there had to some misunderstanding. Mrs. Ramona Dame of White River Junction—with my apologies for saying so in this case—must have been in the wrong when she claimed to have received a letter from Little League Director Angelo 'Bromo' Scelza, in which she was notified that her talented and enthusiastic daughter could not play. Mrs. Dame, in a typical reaction of a distraught mother, claimed discrimination. She then went swiftly to her attorney, a female.

Tactfully, 'Bromo' Scelza refused comment until he knew more. He probably knew that Robin's coach was a staunch and outspoken advocate of the feminist movement and equal rights. After all, when the coach heard about the report he said, "She's a very good hitter, a good fielder and she pitches some. The guys like her and hate to lose her." Advocacy, as noted.

'Bromo' Scelza is reputed to have said, "We have a little problem. Legally, there's nothing to it."

Historically, there's something to this: two years ago, two girls from Quechee participated in the League with no difficulties or comment. So obviously, there was more to this recent matter than members of the skeptical press has presented.

OK, there was a special League meeting, a closed meeting, held last Sunday in the Hartford Municipal Building. But the press reported that there would be a vote on the Robin Dame issue, and that 'Bromo' Scelza "would go along with allowing Robin on the team if other coaches agreed."

More likely the meeting was an affirmation of faith in the basic charter. The fact remains, Scelza laid it right out there after the get-together. He told the press, "The girl will play." More questions from the press. From Scelza: "The girl will play."

'Bromo' did not fizzle out.

A word of warning to followers of this overblown situation. Remember, skeptics never feel obliged to explain things. One of the advantages of being a skeptic is that it enables him to shrink from the obligation which others feel: an obligation to account for all the happenings with truthful explanation—no matter how improbable it may seem.

31

Aunt Rose's Lasting Gift

The Rutland Herald, June 14, 1979

This is strange—to my mind, at least: an introduction that's going to be longer than the original article. But that's because what has been evoked are many, many memories of a woman who defied—still defies—definition. So be it. It's an attempt to extend the borders around the picture drawn in the piece below.

It won't happen again. I promise. And as a gesture of contrition, I've excised from the original article four 'lead-in' paragraphs that seem extraneous now. That won't happen again either.

I am the last witness. My parents and sisters are gone. Aunt Rose is long gone, as are her husband and their two sons. I am the sole carrier forward of Aunt-Rose-lore. What appears below is narrow in focus—inadequate as a representation of a unique woman in our family.

I wrote this piece in 1979 because it was close to my birthday—and it was June. So it reminded me of her—and a very specific story attached to her in perpetuity.

Yes, my introduction to this column will probably pre-empt the column itself. It certainly will give a better look at a woman who, as Willie Nelson sang, "was always on my mind"—and the minds of my parents and siblings. Thoughts of her and stories about her made us happy. So I offer no apologies for this circumstance.

I'll try to present some vignettes about Aunt Rose without launching myself into a biographically excessive tome.

Aunt Rose was 'diminutive' I might say, but I won't. She took up too much space to have that word describe her. She was small, but rotund. Probably a fraction under five feet— and round. Really round. I can't say fat, but I want to. Mrs. Five-by-Five? ("Five feet high and five feet wide," as the song lyrics say.) That's an exaggeration. A more accurate description would be to say that she had the form of the Muppets' Miss Piggy. No exaggeration.

By the husk you may guess the nut. Guess, but not know for sure. And no one knew Aunt Rose 'for sure.' So enough about appearance—for the moment.

She yearned, I believe, to be royalty. Sometimes she acted as if she were. Eccentrically, but not offensively. Someone her size can't 'posture'—she pretends. She says things that hint elitism and that subtly elevate her while diminishing whomever is the object of her gentle disdain. Like the President of the United States. Not always gentle with him. She hated FDR. He was a man of the many, the commoners in our neighborhood said. She was a woman of the few. She had no further explanation of her views; she said she had no use for politics.

What she loved were tea parties (she asked for chocolate; "I have to have some with my tea"), ice-cream socials and luncheon and dinner gatherings. Her first act at table was to turn the chinaware over in her hands to see the maker, decide on the merit of the cup and saucer and, thereby, the hostess. I see her in my mind now as a dealer on the Antiques Road Show, who tells the item owner, "It's fake."

Yet she was kind, in her way, and seemingly un-selfconscious. For example, she sang for years (after it was introduced in 1945 in the Broadway show "Carousel") the song "June is Busting Out All Over," never aware of the laughter, then smiles, it elicited. She sang it only at the canasta or Mah Jongg table, while the games were in progress. The other players never complained. Just laughed, then smiled, then, after a time, just shook their heads in wonder.

You see, Aunty Rose was "busting out all over." Well, not 'all' over exactly. Her clothes (buttons and cloth) strained against the force of tummy and bust. Adding to the general amusement was the belief we all had (even I knew something about it at 10 years of age) that she should have been better corseted, since her husband—my mother's brother—was the chief financial officer at Maidenform. But she kept singing—sometimes humming— 'her song.' Non-stop melody, seemingly; perpetual 'busting out.'

The airs she put on, as if play-acting in a child's performance, provoked me to refer to her, when speaking of her with my sisters (she was a frequent family subject), as "Her Royal Lowness." It evolved to just "Her Lowness"—and it was a little kid's early understanding of irony, based on the disparity between her height and her aspirations.

As I said, she was nice enough, in a distant, off-handed way. Quietly expressing her views of things around her—and, mostly, beyond her. She never let a fact get in the way of her opinion.

Just a harmless, gentle soul who seemed detached from the workings of the world beyond her little, round form. She did raise two boys, both of whom (much older than I) seemed sensible and normal. They served in WW II and brought home souvenirs for me, so their spontaneous gifts were in sharp contrast to Aunt Rose's.

That is a bridge to the article, so I'll cross it now.

Trying to explain (Aunt Rose) is like trying to reach through an electrified fence of words. Nevertheless, the attempt will be made.

There was Aunt Rose and my boyhood desire to have a bulletin board. Aunt Rose, who was eccentric, to say the least, had a reputation for being a gift-giver.

She truly enjoyed the act of giving, and that was fine. Someone once said that it's the will not the gift that makes the giver, and that's where Aunt Rose's eccentricity came in. Her will was to give what pleased *her*, not what might please the recipient. That habit, compounded by her rather unusual tastes, usually made for unenthusiastic recipients.

Just before my seventh birthday, she sent a card to a children's radio personality (Uncle Don was his name) in order to have him broadcast his greetings to me. Uncle Don also told his birthday celebrants where to find a present which he—so he said—had hidden for them.

"Happy Birthday there, Harvey," I heard. "Now look under your bed for a package I've hidden and have a swell time with your present."

"Nonsense!" said Aunt Rose, who had come over to make certain I would listen to the program. (I otherwise would not have.) "*I'm* the one who hid your present!"

I acknowledged the correction and went dutifully to the bedroom. Everyone approached Aunt Rose's gifts with a degree of reluctance. I got down on my hands and knees and, groping in the darkness under the bed, felt a box, which I slid out. Unfortunately, I did not slide my head out so skillfully and was restrained in my attempt to rise by the bed's sideboard, which solidly met the top of my head. Even Aunt Rose had underestimated the impact her present would have on me.

Hours passed, it seemed, before the swelling and the anger subsided. I opened the box. Roller skates! I had, for the most part, been bedridden in those days. Roller skates!!? I hadn't ever roller skated, and there was little prospect of my being able to roller skate in the immediate future.

The electrified fence buzzes. This warning I gave myself: Beware of Aunt Rose bearing gifts.

Yet, to her credit, she was visibly upset about the lump, if not about my face, when I opened the box. It proved to be a fateful emotion; it forced Aunt Rose to step out of character. "You tell me what *you* want most and I shall bring it," she promised.

"A bulletin board!" I screamed without restraint.

She came the next week, unencumbered by any large package. There was no explanation. Each year thereafter, before birthday time—once or twice before Christmas time—she asked if I still wanted a bulletin board. The answer was always a very-resentfully-felt-but-veiled, "Yes." My resentment was as great as it was primarily because no one else, myself included, was permitted to satisfy that deepest of desires, for fear of "offending and hurting dear Aunt Rose because *she* wants to be the one to get you that bulletin board." I'd never get it unless and until Aunt Rose came around and came across.

Twelve years elapsed. No bulletin board. Just prior to my high school graduation Aunt Rose informed me: "It is *time* you had your bulletin board."

My excitement over the announcement had more to do with the abstract meaning than with the tangible gift. The anticipatory joy was unbounded.

But time, I came to find out, is a gypsy. After graduation Aunt Rose presented me with a box of stationery and a Waterman fountain pen.

Dear Aunt Rose,
    May your nose run the way this pen does…

Of course I never sent it.

Of course, I didn't receive the elusive bulletin board. No one ever spoke of it again. It's still better to hope than despair, I decided. Four years later, faint embers still glowed in my obsessive heart. College graduation rekindled thoughts of the impossible.

Aunt Rose and I faced each other afterwards. The silence was poetry. Suddenly, from behind her back, she brought forward—a small box. It was a Bulova watch.

She was dead a week later.

Dear Aunt Rose,
    Had your heart ticked the way the watch does …

To say that part of me died when Aunt Rose died would be like saying …
The electric fence buzzes once again.

32

Three Cheers Please for a Sportswriter

The Rutland Herald, August 2, 1979

The most unusual greeting I'd ever had (or have had since) when I picked up a ringing telephone: "Is this Harvey?"

"Yes."

"You drink scotch?"

"Yes."

"This is Bill Heinz and I have some Johnny Walker Black waiting if you'd care to join me at my house. I read your Herald *piece on Floyd Patterson. Good stuff. I know Floyd well. You did him right."*

And so it started. A first scotch—and many more over the next few years. A relationship that wasn't frequent, but was ongoing. Always at his house; late afternoon. Once a dinner invitation to Anita and me. A pleasant enough evening with Bill and his wife. But it didn't seem to satisfy him, I thought. He had to share the conversation. His interest was in directing the 'conversation'—in doing the talking, in telling, in revealing, explaining, instructing.

And something else, I thought, after a number of one-on-one get-togethers over time. Bill Heinz was a man who had demons (don't we all?). I believe that he could hold them at bay only when he was speaking, telling his stories—because he no could longer ask others for their stories. He had some time ago retired from his work as a writer. He had to silence disturbing inner voices with his own.

In 1946, the legendary Damon Runyon was dying of throat cancer and could scarcely speak. A magazine editor asked him who, in his opinion, was the best young writer in New York. Runyon scrawled the name W.C. Heinz on a cocktail napkin and passed it to him. He had underlined Heinz's name three times. So the story goes.

Manchester Center—Though fully aware that apologies only account for mistakes they can't alter, I offer mine to the reader at the outset. The apology is offered because I know that what I'm going to write in the space available on this page cannot properly tell you what every reader deserves to know about W.C. Heinz. The hours spent talking with him told me more than I can or care to tell you here.

That acknowledgement made, I now suggest a partial remedy: go out and buy the man's latest book, *Once They Heard the Cheers*. You'll understand, I hope.

What you'll understand, and what most struck me during my visits with Bill Heinz at his Dorset home, is the nature of this gentle man, now retired from a tough business. He remains the quintessential professional, a man who never detached himself from his work, and—more significantly—a man who has never detached himself from his humanity.

A self-proclaimed "physical coward," he admired, observed, understood and came to respect the 'physical heroes' he wrote about. A self-proclaimed "manufactured writer," he himself gained the respect of those heroes and of his journalistic colleagues for his skill and professionalism.

Bill Heinz, now 64, unabashedly admits to an early and prolonged love of sport. His body, he always knew, was not the vehicle with which to express this love.

"Not that I was a precocious writer," he explains. "No teacher of mine ever considered my work particularly worthy. But I was persistent. I knew what I wanted to be. I was determined to be a sports writer."

A Middlebury College graduate, Heinz began his journalism career as a copy boy on the old *New York Sun*. During that tenure he came back to Vermont from a visit with his wife-to-be, who was teaching in Montpelier at the time.

"I stopped at *The Rutland Herald* to look for work," he recalls. "There were no positions available."

Fate is the friend of the worthy. Heinz went back to the *Sun* and later distinguished himself as a 'no-name' war correspondent in Europe during WWII. When he returned, the newspaper was ready to reward him for his performance by sending him to Washington, D.C. Thanks, but no thanks, was his essential response. Instead, Heinz asked for and was given a position in the sports department. In the years that followed, he established himself as an eminently successful feature writer and probably the most successful freelancer in the world of sports.

For nearly 20 years his stories about the prominent figures in that world were to be found in *Colliers*, *True*, *Saturday Evening Post* and so on. (*Cosmopolitan* ran a fiction piece of his about a boxer. It was one of their prestigious "Blue Ribbon Award" short stories.) His novel, *The Professional*, remains *the* novel about boxing. His other books were *Run to Daylight*, with and about the legendary Vince Lombardi (and the Green Bay Packers), and two novels about the medical field and its professionals (whom Heinz greatly admires). *The Surgeon* and *Emergency* are the titles. Heinz also ghost wrote the original "*MASH*."

His current book is perhaps his best. Bill Heinz traveled across the country to see, once more, the heroes he had written about years before. It was not a trip for nostalgia's sake, he clarifies. His friend and former colleague, Red Smith of the *Times*, recognizes that the book shouldn't be passed off as just another genre book—"a book about sports." Said Smith, "It is about people who just happened to make their living in sports."

Smith's words were not book jacket casuality. Indeed, in the chapter about Rocky Marciano (who died in a plane crash), it is the heavyweight's mother the reader gets to know better and care more about than her famous son or some of the 'heroes' in other chapters. And she certainly didn't make her living in sports. (Nor did she benefit from any sums made by her sports-hero boy. That is a strange and interesting tale.)

Pete Reiser, Eddie Arcaro, Willie Pep, Joe Page, Willie Davis, Rocky Graziano and a dozen or so other men who had "heard the cheers" are revisited by Heinz, who details in his book how these men's lives have gone since they were at the top of their games. Naturally, there is a diversity of circumstance as there is a range of personality. But the one constant throughout the book—the thread that runs so true—is Bill Heinz, the man. The empathetic, tactful, selfless and sensitive treatment of the hero during and after his prime elevates Heinz as a human, primarily, and as a sports writer, secondarily.

I will take the time and space to provide one example, after all, from a recent talk we had. Heinz told of having had difficulty putting together a magazine story about the highly successful Syracuse University football coach, Ben Schwartzwalder. The coach was reticent and did not seem to perceive what the interviewer was trying to elicit. Heinz kept at him. One night, the writer lay in bed unable to put his body or soul to rest.

"It just wasn't right," remembers Heinz. "'I've got to stop prying into other people's lives,' I said to myself."

The fact remains, Heinz had an impact on the lives of many of his subjects because of the type of person he is, not because he was there 'prying.' He gave guidance to Graziano, among others, and never betrayed a trust for a story. He treated Floyd Patterson with 16-ounce kid gloves while, seemingly, most other writers were bare-knuckling the painfully introverted fighter. Patterson hasn't forgotten. Heinz drove a stricken Pete Reiser cross-country to a hospital, a one-man rescue squad. And more.

Critics are interesting people. Not necessarily nice; not necessarily wise. Interesting. Robert Lipsyte, a former *Times* writer, now a novelist of sorts—and a critic—reviewed *Once They Heard the Cheers* in last week's *Sunday Times Book Review*. Though his piece was generally favorable, a number of misinterpretations were apparent.

"Mr. Heinz's then-and-now portraits are vivid, informative, subtle and moving," wrote Lipsyte. But the reviewer managed to get a misguided shot in just before the bell. Or was it purposefully directed? Whatever the intent, it was a low blow. As part of his final statement, Lipsyte said snidely, "Mr. Heinz, himself, (is) a writer who could find sport in a bayonet charge up the hill..."

Any person—a critic is charitably included—who can read the first chapter of that book and come away with that view is 'interesting,' at best.

When I called Bill on the phone to tell him I'd purchased a copy of the book and wanted to talk with him after I finished reading it, he apologized because I had to "pay so much for it." ($12.95) That's the kind of guy he is.

The book was worth the cost. That's the kind of writer he is.

Postscript—Heinz was a five-time winner of the E.P. Dutton Award for best magazine story of the year. He won the A. J. Libeling Award for outstanding boxing writing, and his work has been reprinted in more than 60 anthologies and textbooks. He was inducted into the National Association of Sportscaster and Sportswriters Hall of Fame in 2001 and into the International Boxing Hall of Fame in 2004. In 2008 the Associated Press Sports Editors posthumously awarded him the Red Smith Award for his contributions to sports journalism.

Bill told me he was "quite comfortable" (financially) during his retirement, thanks to the residual payments he received "every time they run one of those blessed M*A*S*H shows on TV in all of the Podunks across America."

Wilfred Charles Heinz died in Bennington, Vermont, on February 27, 2008. He was 93 years old.

33

There She Goes,
His Ideal—and Hope

The Rutland Herald, August 16, 1979

I was sitting at my desk at the Herald, *flipping through the pages of the day's edition. All kinds of flippable stuff: Miss America Pageant coming up in the foreseeable future, blurbs about the upcoming election and the Governors' anxiety over re-election. But mostly I was wondering about a topic for my next "Miscellany" column.*

Hey, wait a minute: Miss America; Miss Vermont; Mr. Governor. Miss Vermont had never become a Miss America; that much I knew. What a boon for the Governor if he could bask in the spotlight of such an eventuality—sharing it with the lovely winner, of course. Could he do anything to help bring it off? That much I fantasized over.

So, after doing some research, grabbing the phone and calling Miss Vermont, I launched my little game: a one-act, two scene play with a little truth and a lot of fiction and loads of fun—for me. It covered three full pages of the Thursday edition—exotic with graphics.

SCENE I

(Setting: The office of the Governor of Vermont. The Governor sits at his desk wearing a countenance of weary concern slightly masked by a thin veil of optimism. He peers over the top of his Ben Franklin spectacles at his executive assistant, with whom the Governor has been discussing, at agonizing length, recent developments within the state and the concomitant problems. The executive assistant has convinced his superior that the popularity of the Governor has been plummeting. The masses—the voters—are disenchanted as the 1980 election draws dangerously close. Both men have agreed that a dramatic distraction, a winning image-enhancer, must be conceived if positive public opinion is to be re-affirmed and the Governor re-elected.

The Governor, himself, gave birth to the thought being discussed; his subordinate has been less than enthusiastic. The idea, in the Governor's words, "is to leave no log unturned, and to go all out to bring a winner home from the upcoming Miss America Pageant in Atlantic City."

As these words are spoken, the curtain rises.

Gov.—I tell you it's a disgrace. A Miss Vermont has never even been close to winning anything at the Miss America contest! How many years have these things been going on with Miss Vermont being a perennial loser?

Asst.—Since 1921, I think. But I believe a Rutland girl won something twenty years ago.

Gov.—Never!

Asst.—Yes, a Miss USA, about twenty years ago.

Gov.—Was Bert Parks there? Did he sing, "There she goes, my ideal …"? Did millions of people all over this country watch it and cry? Was it Miss America?

Asst.—No.

Gov.—Then she won nothing!

Asst.—But, Governor, what makes you think a Vermont girl's winning of that thing can be politically profitable to us, er, you? Miss America? After all…

Gov.—State pride! Morale! Use your imagination, boy. I'd be the first governor of this great state to have that feather in a felt hat. A winner! Miss America *from Vermont!!* I've been thinking about this, boy. I remember Lt. Gov. Burgess at Miss Vermont's farewell dinner in 1974. Puffing up real close to her for a newspaper picture. He was no dope. Wanted to be Governor.

Asst.—It didn't seem to help him.

Gov.—'Course not; Tom Salmon was the honored guest. Seeking re-election, boy. Get the parallel? Why there were more candidates and wives at that Elks Club dinner than there were friends of Donna Shea. A character was there who was just running for country deputy sheriff.

Asst.—Did *he* win?

Gov.—Don't know, but I do know Donna Shea didn't. Nice girl in Vermont, but a loser in Atlantic City.

Asst.—What do you propose to do, set up a State Agency for the Development and Beautification of Vermont Females?

Gov.—Look here, Jim, the past losers, except for the most recent three, are not on *my* head. And I'm not looking to set up anything for any future governor. I just want to win in 1980. We have only a short time in which to operate—for Miss Vermont and for me, er, us.

Asst.—When is the contest held?

Gov.—Pageant. We have to start calling it 'pageant.' The final night—Bert Parks and company—is Saturday, September 8 at Convention Hall, Atlantic City, New Jersey. Millions of TV viewers.

Asst.—You established that point already. How do you know so much about this business?

Gov.—Yes, it's *your* job to fill *me* in on details, isn't it?

Asst.—I didn't think these details were part of my responsibility yet, or of our mutual interest. I'll bone up on the subject.

Gov.—Flesh up, you mean. (Laughter)

Asst.—Whatever you say. What shall I do in the meantime?

Gov.—First, get in touch with Miss Vermont, 1979. I want to talk with her. Before that I'll have you fill me in on her background.

Asst.—And foreground, I assume.

Gov.—(Laughter) Sure, sure. Second, get a hold of the Attorney General. Have him check into the honesty and authenticity of the selection process down there in Boardwalk town. Have him go back three years, you never know. Look at what happened with that Miss Universe contest a month or so ago. Everybody knew the winner before the show was on the air. Probably rigged, and we don't want that to happen to us.

Asst.—Wasn't that held in Australia?

Gov.—So you know more than you admit?

Asst.—Well, I was kind of high on Miss Guatemala.

Gov.—Oh brother, thank goodness no one asked you to judge the Miss Vermont contest in Middlebury.

Asst.—Pageant.

Gov.—It's not a pageant unless Bert Parks is there. Remember that. Anyhow, have Jerry check out any possible discrimination. We're a small state and some of those judges never even heard of us way up here.

Asst.—Don't southern girls usually win it?

Gov.—Aagh, I can just hear them drawling their spontaneous answers to the sealed questions, "Ah jest hope ta make ma country a betta place in which we kin live peece-ably an' har*moan*iosly an' democratically, y'all heea. Amen."

Asst.—(Laughter)

Gov.—It's no laughing matter, Jim. Get after it. We've got only three weeks to take matters in our hands—as much as we can.

Asst.—Yes, sir. (Exits)

Curtain falls. End of Scene I.

SCENE II

(Setting: Again, in Governor's office. The Governor sits behind his desk, now with more relaxed facial configurations. He is erect in his chair, his posture purposeful and anticipatory. It has been two days since the Governor's meeting with his executive assistant and the formation of a strategy pertaining to the Miss America Pageant. The assistant's arrival is announced on the Governor's intercom as the curtain rises.)

Gov.—Send him in. (Enter assistant) Well, Jim, how about a full report?

Asst.—Good morning, Governor.

Gov.—Oh yes, good morning, Jim.

Asst.—To begin, Jerry's investigating the recent history of the pageant concerning its honesty, as you suggested.

Gov.—Three years. We needn't spend the taxpayers' money by going back any farther.

Asst.—Of course not. Also, I've sent detectives out to check the background of this year's judges.

Gov.—Good work. I assume you checked the detectives' backgrounds first. Where did you get the judges' names?

Asst.—I'd rather not reveal my sources, Governor.

Gov.—I understand. What are you looking for particularly?

Asst.—Oh, causes for people to be resentful or discriminatory or hostile toward Vermont or Vermonters. A skier, perhaps, who got a speeding ticket in Vermont; someone related to a whey plant malcontent or a state policeman; a guy, maybe, who had a trauma on the Alpine Slide; someone who might once have tried to ask directions in the Northeast Kingdom; a democrat; anything I can think of.

Gov.—Good, good!

Asst.—Also, I have someone from WCAX-TV going over tapes I acquired from NBC to see if camera shots have been the same for everyone in the past—when contestants are on the stage, you know. In other words, does our Miss Vermont always get the bad shaft of light and all the poor angles?

Gov.—And have them made more obvious!

Asst.—No, no, I didn't mean our girls' angles, I meant the camera... You've got the idea, right? And of course ...

Gov.—Only the past three years.

Asst.—Check. And as you wished, I contacted Miss Vermont, 1979, got some background and have her waiting outside right now.

Gov.—Very fine, but first let me hear a bit so I can be direct with the young lady. Is she a winner? Does she *want* to win? Does she know her responsibility to me, er, to the glorious state of Vermont?

Asst.—She's a lovely girl.

Gov.—They're ALL *lovely girls*. I'm tired of *lovely girls*. I want a Miss America, lovely or not! (He pounds the desk, then abruptly regains his composure.) Is the tape off? (Fumbles under his desk) Yes. (Pause) What's her name?

Asst.—Shari Bach.

Gov.—Is that all? I mean, I was hoping for another name. I mean an additional name, like Lee Ann Merriwether.

Asst.—Well, her middle name happens to be Lee.

Gov.—Terrific! That sounds more southern. (Sarcastically) Where was she born, in Shaftsbury?

Asst.—She happens to have been born in the deeper South, but she's been living in Middlebury for ...

Gov.—Really born down south! Double terrific! Bach, huh. Any relation to Johann Sebastian? (Laughter)

Asst.—That I couldn't tell you, but she is a piano teacher.

Gov.—Wonderful! Wait a minute. Did you say teacher? How old is she, 52?

Asst.—The range for eligibility in the pageant is 17-26. She's 22. Still, one of the older contestants.

Gov.—Piano, you say. They say talent holds some sway in the pageant, though I don't believe it for a minute.

Asst.—Talent is the number one consideration, ahead of the spontaneous response, ahead of personality, gown and ...

Gov.—Don't say it... bathing suit? (The assistant gives an affirmative nod.) Well, then, our Shari Lee Bach had better play her piano for all she's worth... Hold on. She better play her piano, period. She *is* going to play the piano, right? Don't tell me she's going to reform by jumping around on a trampoline or whistling or being a ventriloquist. And she better not act out a skit she wrote. Someone did that last year, I remember, and ...

Asst.—Miss Vermont did.

Gov. (Slapping his head) What? Good grief, I should have supervised this business three years ago. Run it, in fact.

Asst.—Actually, Miss Vermont's father wrote the skit.

Gov.—Oh, wonderful. Enough. Bring this year's girl in.

(The executive assistant rises, leaves the room momentarily and returns with Miss Vermont, who is holding the assistant's arm, which is held in chivalric rigidity. The Governor leaps from behind his desk and grasps Miss Vermont's hand, which he shakes vigorously.)

Gov.—Glad to meet you, Miss Vermont.

M.V.—Miss Bach, sir.

Gov.—Yes, of course, Miss Bach.

M.V.—You may call me Shari, sir.

Gov.—May I call you Shari Lee?

M.V.—Yes, of course, sir.

Gov.—You may call me Governor.

M.V.—Yes, of course, Governor.

Gov.—Sit down, my dear. (She does.) Now Shari Lee, we're here to talk about winning the whole ball of wax—the crown—this year, y'all hear? I mean, do you understand? This is not a no-win state and I am not a no-win guy and you will not be a no-win girl. Miss Vermont has been getting clobbered year after year, since 1921 in the Miss America Pageant. In front of millions of people, including Bert Parks. It's time for a winner!

Asst.—At least a finalist, Shari.

Gov.—A WINNER, Shari Lee!

Asst.—We did win Miss Congeniality, Governor, In 1956. Sandra Simpson.

Gov.—The hell with Miss Congeniality! (He fumbles with his hand under the desk, then calms himself.) Sorry, Miss V,. er, Shari Lee. Now Shari Lee, let's get an unpleasant question over with first: What happened to your growth, dear?

M.V.—I can't say, Governor. I'm only 5'3" but when I have heels on I look like a lady. I get up to 5'5" and ...

Gov.—Has anyone this short ever won, Jim?

Asst.—No, sir, but last year's Miss Vermont was the tallest girl in the pageant, 5'11"—and that didn't seem to help us, er, her, er, you.

Gov.—Call your man at WCAX-TV and tell him to be in New Jersey when the time comes. We want him standing right next to the NBC cameraman to make sure the guy knows Shari Lee's whereabouts while she's out there. I mean I want him to find her down that low. Now Shari Lee, I assume—I hope—you're going to play the piano during the talent segment.

M.V.—Yes, Governor.

Gov.—You're not going to play "Galveston, Oh Galveston," or something like that?

M. V.—No, Governor. A prelude by Grieg from a little suite he wrote.

Gov.—Speak up, dear, I can hardly hear you. Practice here. *Emote*! Let your personality show through. Now Shari Lee, how long does the piece run?

M.V.—Oh, a minute and a half to two minutes, depending on my mood.

Gov.—Good mood, dear, good mood. Go at the piece. Defeat it. Bring it to its knees! What kind of background will you have? A big orchestra?

M.V.—I could have, Governor. I had a choice. I chose to play solo. Then I have no one to blame but myself.

Gov.—To praise, not to blame, dear. Be aggressive; be positive!

M.V.—I do have a lot of confidence in myself and my talent, sir. But it seems to be different from what you have in mind. Actually, I entered the Miss Vermont pageant at the suggestion of a friend. The talent part was my main interest, and winning a scholarship, which I've already done. But it was hard for me to accept that I'd been chosen. They had to push me out when my name was called.

Gov.—(Holding his head) But ... but you're a pretty little thing. Why were you surprised?—Don't answer that. Tell me your measurements.

M.V.—I'm not sure, really.

(The Governor's eyes dart toward his assistant.)

Asst.—34-25-33.

M.V.—(Smiling) I've been called 'squatty body.'

Gov.—(Holding head again) Now let's change the subject, Shari Lee. I know you're 22 years old. When did you graduate from Middlebury High School?

M.V.—I didn't. I never formally attended school.

Gov.—Jim, get me a couple of aspirin. Get me a drink …

Asst.—Governor, relax a minute. Shari's father was a writer and designer. Her family traveled around a lot, so the father decided to have her tutored instead of putting her in schools. Don't worry, she knows more than the graduates who'll be in Atlantic City.

Gov.—Shari Lee, I want you to try to read as many of the Harvard Classics as you can between now and pageant time.

Asst.—Governor, Shari has read. And she attended the Eastman School of Music.

M.V.—I've also done some course work at the University of Texas.

Gov.—Texas? Good, good. Tell Bert Parks that; you never know, the word might spread. Let everybody hear it. But Shari Lee, watch your mouth. I mean, use your head when they ask you that individual question. Jim, read what Miss Vermont said last year.

Asst.—(Reluctantly opens his notebook) She said, "Some of my best friends are gay and I …"

Gov.—Please now, dearie, don't …

Asst.—There's more, Governor. It explains her point.

Gov.—That's quite enough to make *my* point.

M.V.—Governor, don't worry about my poise. I'm older than most of the other girls and can handle it. I feel the difference in age. When the New England winners gathered in Boston, I felt like a mother to the other girls.

Gov.—Good grief, I'm not talking about Grandma America—or poise, either. I'm talking about controversy, purity, image. Winning! What if the question is, let's see—What is your dream for the future? That's it. Answer me. What is your dream for the future?

M.V.—My dream for the future is to have a business of my own. A music business.

Gov.—You don't have to say you want to save the world, but couldn't you at least say you want to write songs for the handicapped? A business? Is that what you'd tell them if they asked?

M.V. Yes. And I'll tell you this: I'm going to go down there and have lots of fun, play my music and enjoy the experience. I don't expect to win. That was never my dream. Actually, I feel sorry for those girls who take it so seriously. But I won't put on an act for anyone.

Gov.—So that's our ball of wax, is it?

M.V.—Well, Governor, it surely is *my* ball of wax—and this has been a pleasant experience talking with you. (Rises) I really must be going now.

(The assistant escorts her to the door.)

Gov.—One last thing before you leave, Shari Lee. Win or lose, do me a big favor.

M.V.—I'll try, Governor. What is it?

Gov.—Please don't let the other girls name you Miss Congeniality.

M.V.—Hell no, sir! (She closes the door behind her.)

Asst.—Nice girl, sir.

Gov.—(Nodding his head distractedly) Real nice, real nice. (Pause) Jim, I've got a new plan …

Asst.—Why don't we wait until after September 9, Governor? Who can tell …?

Gov.—Maybe that's right, Jim. Maybe that's right.

Curtain falls.

THE END—

Postscript—The next day's edition of the Herald *included an editorial written by the paper's owner/publisher, a kindly old fellow who, in retrospect, was probably hanging around the borders of dotage. In the editorial, he lambasted the Governor of Vermont for behavior that was cynical, clumsy, callous and degrading to his office—or words to that effect. I never saw the commentary.*

I did see—on the same editorial page the following day—my editor's response to the publisher's remarks, and possibly to other outrages that came across his desk. In a small box below the other editorials, this explanation from Steve Terry, Managing Editor:

FICTION

A piece on state officials and beauty queens appearing Thursday on the Southern Vermont Living pages was a spoof on bureaucracy and was fiction. A number of people thought it was a transcript of a conversation at a government policy-making session.

34

A Father Gives His Young Son a Lesson, and Also Learns One

The New York Times, August 26, 1979

The editor of the Times *Sunday sports page was very kind to me. Oh, I'm sure it wasn't pure altruism. He had an ulterior motive: to fill the page with what he liked. And he told me he liked the whimsical baseball stuff that included my children, "so send along another such piece some time." The previous piece I'd done for him in this genre was in 1975. A few serious offerings had been printed in the interim.*

My son's timing was impeccable. My surprise—at his heightened interest in baseball—was palpable. My piece was waiting to be written.

"Can you believe that Mickey Rivers got traded?" my son asked. My own incredulity at his asking was great, my pride greater still.

I guess the time had come for me to boast about what seems to have been a highly successful behavior modification program. The purpose was to change a son's attitude toward baseball from apathy to enthusiasm. His first love, you see, is ornithology.

I initiated the program more than five years ago, after he had humiliated me (and my 1945 New York Giants) in a baseball table game. I had taken the defeat with little grace but with considerable hope—hope that his taste for the real game of baseball might be tantalized. For a long time, it wasn't.

Last year's strategy, based on two aspects of his personality—a competitive spirit and an immoderate interest in money—precipitated my major breakthrough.

THE 3-PLAYER, 6-HIT POOL

I made the first big move right off the bat, during the opening weekend of the 1978 season. My 15-year-old daughter, who loves baseball (bless her), was employed as a collaborator. While my 12-year-old son was within earshot, my daughter listened attentively as I tripped nostalgically back to 1949, when bookies in my high school ran what was then known in the Bronx as three-player, six-hit pools. I explained loudly that interested individuals would select three players on a given day, the aim being to have one's picks get six hits, cumulatively, during that day's action. The bookmaker gave 3-1 odds against the bettor's intelligence—or luck.

"Three-to-what for *what?*" my son asked. The explanation was repeated with a feigned casual air.

"Care to give it a try?" I asked. He turned toward his sister and signaled with a nod of his head. They disappeared upstairs.

MUSIAL, WILLIAMS, KELL, ET. AL.

I reclined in my chair. Visions of players and payoffs danced in my head. The 1949 vintage standard choices: Musial, Williams, Kell, Robinson, Doerr, *et. al.* And my own esoteric "money players": Elmer Valo, Cass Michaels, Bob Dillinger of the old St. Louis Browns, and the 42-year-old shortstop, Luke Appling, who hit .301 in the 1949 regular season and .435 in my pools.

Yesterday's box scores disappeared with the reappearance of my daughter. "Where's Danny?" I whispered.

"Just finishing poking through my baseball cards," she said (bless her).

Presently, he came into the room. "Are you the guy who gives the odds?" he asked directly.

"I am."

"OK. Is this for today?"

It was the season's first Sunday—April 9; a full schedule was to be played. I nodded my assent and repeated the odds, lest the fish not swallow the hook.

"For how much?" he asked.

"Make it easy on yourself."

"Fifty cents."

"Big hitter," I said. "Who are your players?"

"Gamblecashmoney," he fired back rapidly.

My face showed obvious lack of understanding.

"Oscar Gamble, Dave Cash and Don Money," my daughter pronounced slowly.

"Very symbolic," I said, but by that time Danny was out the door looking for bird nests.

JACKSON, CAREW, CEDENO

"May I try too?" asked my daughter. I hadn't even given the prospect a thought, but naturally I didn't refuse. Basic choices for Melissa: Reggie Jackson, Rod Carew and Cesar Cedeno. I pursed my lips in a sign of respect.

The following evening we reconvened over the Monday sports page. Melissa's players had collected a total of nine hits. She was paid off. We scanned the box scores for Danny's choices.

"Here's Money," I said. Three hits. Gamble, two. Oh, oh. Cash didn't get any. Too bad; I'm afraid you're a loser this time."

Danny glanced over my shoulder and pointed. "Wait a minute," he said, his other hand raised. It says his name again here—Cash, and the one hit that I need, if this is the right column."

It was. The Expos had played a doubleheader. I tried to explain Bronx rules, but his claim was that I had said nothing about how many games.

$21.75 LATER

"Same deal next week, I hope." he said, pocketing his profits.

"Maybe so," I answered, with a hope of my own.

"By the way," he remembered on the way out of doors once more, "the phoebes are back nesting across from your bedroom window."

"Dad's only interested in Blue Jays, Cardinals and Orioles, Danny," shouted my daughter (bless her).

Now, a year later, ornithology still has a secure grip on first place in Danny's heart. But baseball has moved ahead of matchbox cars into second. He even knows who's playing center field for the Yankees. Six years and $21.75 were all it took.

35

The Lone Ranger's Call
Heard Clearly Here

The Rutland Herald, August 30, 1979

I had hoped to crack the op-ed page of The New York Times. *I thought I had a good vehicle for it: a story that had just broken—more human absurdity, a recurrent theme. It hit close to home—if home truly is where the heart is.*

As a very young boy, most of my days were spent in bed, listening to the radio and reading books. The radio fare, aside from baseball games, was music, afternoon soap operas and evening adventure programs. My favorite was "The Lone Ranger." My familiarity with this heroic fellow was expanded through Lone Ranger books and, later, television. (I had a set in my bedroom when I was ten years old; that would be in 1945.) I knew the man; I revered the man.

And now, according to the newspaper report I read, the man himself (well, the man who played the man himself) was being abused and humiliated. I had to come to the rescue.

Professionally speaking, I was too late. At least when it came to crashing the Times op-ed page. I received a kind letter from the page's editor saying that he very much liked my article, but that Russell Baker, "our (elite) columnist who appears regularly on the page, had submitted his column—on the same subject. Try us again." (I did, a year-and-a-half later, with success.)

A fiery horse with the speed of light, a cloud of dust and hearty, 'Hi Yo, Silver! The Lone Ranger rides again!

Eternal youth. That's justice.

Nothing improves with age, apparently. Or endures. Ask the masked man. The unmasked man, actually. A deciduous, defrocked hero.

Hero? Our corporations and courts have never heard of the word. The memory of a great name? Bah! The inheritance of a great example? We have sent in the clowns.

115

The Lone Ranger has peeled life like an onion, and now they will have him weep.

Texas Ranger John Reid was out riding with his brother, Captain Dan Reid, and four other Rangers. The six men were ambushed by Butch Cavendish and his Hole-in-the-Wall gang at Bryant's Gap. Thanks to the aid of an Indian named Tonto, John Reid was brought back to life, so to speak. He was the sole survivor. John asked the red man if brother Dan was still alive.

Tonto replied, "All others dead; you the Lone Ranger now."

John made a vow and a mask. The cloth for the mask came from his dead brother's vest.

With his faithful Indian companion, Tonto, the daring and resourceful masked rider of the plains led the fight for law and order in the early western United States.

That history is a voice which will sound from those plains across forever. It will ring out the laws of right and wrong. Opinions alter, manners change, creeds rise and fall, but the codes of justice are written on the tablets of eternity.

Present circumstances, however, add up to an eternal now, and the clowns are making it a vulgar epoch.

That the public good be served. *That* is justice.

Nowhere in the annals of history can we find a greater champion of justice.

Clayton Moore has been the Lone Ranger for 30 years on radio and television and in films. He doesn't say exactly how old he is (the Lone Ranger should remain a bit reticent), but the guess is he's between 65 and 70. Great champions are prohibited from getting old.

The great masked champion has been unmasked. It seems the rights to the 'character' were bought in 1954 for $3 million by Lone Ranger Television, Inc., a subsidiary of Wrather Corp. The company is planning a new Lone Ranger film. Needless to say, the plan does not include Clayton Moore.

Not satisfied with that affront, the corporation has gone to court to completely strip Moore of his Lone Rangership. They can't. We all know Moore is THE Lone Ranger. The corporation's action is an unctuous gesture that good citizens can only deplore.

Had it understood social history, the corporation would have planned a movie based on Lone Ranger progeny. *Son of the Lone Ranger*, for example. Perhaps, *Daughter of the Lone Ranger*. Or *The Sound of Rangers*.

Adding insolence to insult, and interdiction to injury, the corporation further asked the courts to forbid Moore from wearing his mask in public and telling people (as if they didn't really know) that he is the mysterious masked man. Spokesman for the company said Moore has "gained weight' and "his skin is getting loose."

Corporate lawyers, yes; poets, no.

"But in the flesh (beauty) is immortal. The body dies; the body's beauty lives."

They stopped short of declaring him senile, but they said his public appearances undercut promotional campaigns for the new film. Moore, they said, no longer is an "appropriate physical representative of the … Western hero."

No sense of definition, no sense of symbolic reality, no sense of respect for the aged.

The courts listened; the courts issued an injunction against Moore.

No sense at all. That is justice.

The Lone Ranger can no longer make public appearances, for which he had been paid peanuts for himself, oats for his horse—just what Ralph Waldo Emerson received for his public presentations. Henry Kissinger is given $25,000 for his appearances and utterances.

A nose of wax. That is justice.

Where is Britt Reid, alias the Green Hornet, great-grand-nephew of the Lone Ranger? Not heard from during this time of family crisis.

And where is Tonto, who should be at the sole survivor's side once more, aiding, consoling, lest the pulsating sounds of Rossini's "William Tell Overture" be muted? Tonto is probably hanging out at 6925 Hollywood Boulevard, waiting to stick his moccasin in the wet cement in front of Grauman's Chinese Theater.

Leaving the Lone Ranger, in alleged dotage, to bite the silver bullet alone. What then will we hear, Verdi's "Requiem"?

That no one shall suffer wrong. That is justice.

Memory is the only place from which we can't be turned out.

Return with us now to those thrilling days of yesteryear. From out of the past come the thundering hoofbeats of the great horse, Silver. The Lone Ranger rides again!

Justice triumphs, Kemo Sabe.

Postscript—I sheepishly report that my comments about Tonto's abandonment were out of order. A Vermonter named Emily Jennsion wrote to me, kindly saying she thought my piece to be "superior to Russell Baker's." She included in her note the fact that she learned of the Lone Ranger's unmasking, "this awful event, on TV—and (saw) there by his (the Lone Ranger's) side … his faithful companion, Tonto." The writer added, "I thought you'd like to know this."

Emily, in the name of justice for Tonto, I am very happy to hear of it. Thanks to you— and my apologies to the faithful companion.

36

From the Armchair of
Harvey Dorfman

The Rutland Herald, September 12, 1979

A small state; a big pride. So it was understandable how proud Vermonters felt when one of their own, Stella Hackel, was named Director of the U.S. Mint. But the lofty sentiment would come crashing down like the spilt sack of coins responsible for the terrible circumstance. A sack full of Susan B. Anthony dollars, introduced by Stella Hackel. The coin that was to become a state embarrassment and a national debacle.

With this piece I returned to the format of 'the Dorfman Letter' (though I certainly would have chosen a title other than the one chosen by the paper's 'slug man'). My intention was to write to "Mrs. H.," as one of her fellow Green Mountain Boys (yes, she's a female: I know), and let her know that I am in on her joke. Surely, I knew she couldn't be serious about the coin and was having a romp in Washington while she had the chance. That's what I told her with a wink and a nod. We Vermonters, after all, understood each other.

The Postscript *provides a retrospective glimpse—history—of the coin itself: a disastrous one, at that. At least, as it affected the status of one Vermonter.*

Stella Hackel, Director
U.S Bureau of the Mint
Washington, D.C.

Dear Mrs. H.,

By golly, I had to write this note to tell you what a grand time I'm havin' watchin' a Vermont girl makin' monkeys out of people in the U.S. capital. I should actually say makin' people all across the U.S. of America go foolish over your Susan Anthony one-dollar piece. I know you're havin' as big a laugh over the fuss as I am, and I'm sure we're joined by a flock of other Yankees who understand your Green Mountain sense of humor. At least I hope so. It's a wonderful joke, and sooner or later the rest of the country will catch up with your wit. Meanwhile, we're proud of you back home.

I read in the local paper that you're gettin' ready to take a trip across the continent to "promote the use of the coin..." I wish I could be a fly on your purse when you're repeating those words you said about the Suzie dollar bein' a "successful coin because it's a useful item."

I like how, for good measure, you told 'em, "It makes sense." Pretty good, Mrs. H., pretty good. But remember; don't crack a smile if you're in front of those media people when you're saying that. They'll smell rotten cabbage right off. You know how they look for trouble. Well, they'll be lookin' special hard, because one of your lady friends in Washington, Mary Rose Okar from Ohio, I think, blabbed out that "the media didn't give it (the dollar) a chance."

I hope you've clued her in on the joke, Mrs. H. Still, the media gang doesn't forget that kind of talk, I'm told. So be on your toes; be sophisticated, as they say down in Boston.

I'll say this, it sure has helped that you go around wearin' those sports designer spectacles and all that gold jewelry. It's a swell idea. No one will ever suspect you're a Vermonter; ergo, no one will ever suspect you're a leg-puller.

By golly, you must be happy as a clam at high water and havin' a time-and-a-half. Imagine, a few years back you wanted to be Governor of our state. I'm sure you'd be disappointed as wet gun powder if you had to trade jobs with our fella back here now. Not for all the gold in Fort Knox, right, Mrs. H.? (We still have some of that stuff left, don't we? I hope so.)

Well, well. Just think what you've been able to do with your new coin that everyone is hatin' and refusin' to use. You've cancelled out quite a few smart folks' ideas about the American dollar, you have. Such as Washington Irving's. He called the dollar a "great object of universal devotion throughout our land." Those days of greed are over, right, Mrs. H.?

My Uncle Oscar used to say, "The dollar is a friend that'll open all the doors you could want." The joke would be on him if he wasn't dead as the Roman Empire.

"A piece of green paper having healing properties." A double knee-slapper, that one. I don't recall who the wiseacre was.

And finally, a real smarty named Elbert Hubbard, from Maine, but I'm not sure as eggs on it, said the dollar was "a sacred object, contact with which is looked upon as a curative and prophylactic." That's a mite uppity for Maine and for me, but I do know the Suzie dollar will make Elbert swallow that potato with considerable difficulty.

Now then, have you heard the story about the lady who got angry at a restaurant supplier? It's clean, Mrs. H., and it's true. Happened down near where you're at. It seems the lady didn't like a businessman's attitude. She went to buy an icebox—I guess you know it as a refrigerator—with her husband. It was for their general store—I guess you know it as a delicatessen. Somewhere in Virginia. The gent told the lady, "I don't deal with women." Well, come to find out they bought the equipment, all right, but she made sure to pay the fella off in 3,000 fresh-minted Sue Anthony coins. (It seems Sue was a big shot lady-libber back when.)

So much for stories. You must have heard 'em all: how the banks are grumblin' about the coins and the department stores are sayin' they never see 'em, because nobody wants to be caught carryin' one. I truly got a bolt out of the way you pretended to get mad about all the talk over the coin's size. You know, how they say your dollar's just like a quarter. I read this. Did you really say it? I hope so.

"Look, look. They're not alike! Look at them. They're not like quarters."

Then you got rollin', it seems. You held one right in your pink palm and said (I hope), "It's 43 percent heavier. It has a raised inner border. There's a woman on the face instead of a man. They're just not alike."

Like a fox on a poultry farm, Mrs. H. I bet they were swallowed up by it. I sure hope so.

And I hope I don't embarrass you when I tell you I think it's downright genius to call in those public relations boys like you did. Could they be the same boys who did the work for Edsel? If you have a sluggish moment, ask 'em what they think of this pitch: "Send in one Sue, and we'll send you back two." I tried it out on my wife first. She liked it: no charge if they use it. My pleasure.

I also thought you might tell the federal fellas to make Chrysler Corp. take a barge of Suzies. It'll serve 'em right.

Anyhow, I see a New York firm has already put out a nice and bright little color booklet for you: "The Dollar of the Future." Tell me you wrote at least *part* of it, Mrs. H. The part that says the new coin is "easy to hear if dropped.," and "unlike bills, won't stick together when new or tear when old." Tell me, Mrs. H., tell me. Clever as paint.

I'll tell you, I don't know where it all ends for our girl from Vermont. It's excitin' meanwhile. You've told people the Suzie will last about ten times as long as a paper dollar, and I believe it will. You've said the coins will last 15 or more years, but I believe they'll last as long as an undertaker's face, if you know what I mean, and I believe you do, Mrs. H.

You sure knew what that study group called into action by the federal Reserve Bank meant when it said that for your coin to be a success, "the $1 bill must be withdrawn from circulation." It said, "At no time did we find a participant in the currency system that felt the $1 coin and the $1 bill could successfully coexist."

You were as eager as a ghoul for blood, you were. "That's (a) research project, period. It may or may not be valid," you said.

Best be careful, Mrs. H. That didn't sound like typical Yankee wisdom. Don't let 'em get to you; play the joke out. Tell 'em you'll get rid of the bills entirely, if that's the way it's got to be. Don't quit just yet, Mrs. H.

Well, this is gettin' to sound like advice, and that's the smallest coin there is, they say. So let me close out this message with an interestin' (I hope) piece of history. It tells me more than the Farmer's Almanac can. What it tells me is that you're a U.S. woman of destiny now.

Listen here. One hundred years ago—exactly—the Treasury struck a $4 coin. Only about 400 of 'em were minted, not like the billions you'll be into and up to. The name of that 1879 coin was—get this—"Stella." By gosh, that's what it was called, and I think history is repeatin' itself.

Why just the other day I heard one of our tourists callin' your coin "Stella's Folly," though I can't be sure he gets the entire joke. Close enough, by golly. Whether it's "Suzie" or "Stella," you'll be remembered for this fine Yankee prank (I hope), and by gosh you deserve it.

My neighbor was sayin' that "money is like manure; no value less'n it's spread." Well, I explained your romp to him and now I think he's appreciatin' it. At any rate (that's a little word joke, I hope), I am.

Numismatically yours,

H.A. Dorfman

P.S. By the by, just in case this coin isn't a bit of fun on your part, please forward the address of the U.S. Patent Office to me, if you're so kind. I've got plans drawn up for an invention that takes, holds and ejects back your dollars. It'll replace the billfold, surely. I've got a yen to get the patent out before the Japanese folks, and that's no joke.

H.A.D.

Postscript—One may not need to know all this, but I thought it should be offered, lest the reader not see both sides of the coin.

The Susan B. Anthony silver dollar is considered to be one of the most unpopular coins in American history. The origin design called for the coin to be a hendecagon (11-sided curve), but vending machine manufacturers rebelled against the plan, saying that available technology would require extensive and expensive retooling to accommodate the irregular shape of the coin.

The coin was frequently (almost always?) mistaken to be a quarter. The original plan to have it be hendecagon-shaped would have distinguished it from the quarter. But that design was scrapped. It ended up having the same appearance as a quarter and the same reeded edge, thus causing the great confusion.

It was released July 2, 1979—and much of the criticism for it fell on the President of the United States, rather than on Stella Hackel. (It was often referred to as the "Carter quarter.") A large quantity was produced in 1979, but they did not circulate well at all—despite a desperate PR attempt to stimulate circulation. ("Carry three for Susan B.") A minimal number were produced the following year. In 1981, none were produced for circulation.

At the end of production, the Treasury vaults were stuffed with hundreds of millions of the coins.

Stella Hackel took her stuff and left office that year—1981—moving to Arlington, Virginia—not to Vermont.

37

Real Hearts Have Their Reasons

The New York Times, February 14, 1981

I had the opportunity to land a piece on the Times *op-ed page. That was fun. Reading it again now, I am struck by the thought that it landed there more because of moment than merit. The topicality, which is always a key for being able to appear on the page, was one I decided to take advantage of. So there I was—on Valentine's Day.*

Perhaps some people enjoyed reading it.

Manchester Center, Vt.—Invariably, at this time of year, I become aware of a recurring, pleasant sensation in the middle of my chest. It is identifiable and very familiar: a convergence of genes about my heart. My father's genes, surely.

A man who believed that custom was a tyrant—and who pretended that the display of emotion was one of man's baser instincts—my father, nevertheless, set aside Valentine's Day as his own personal holiday. The more popularly and officially proclaimed days of celebration he would "observe" by, for example, picking out a cemetery plot.

But Valentine's Day was quite another story.

It seemed to represent a paradox of personality. He never bothered to discuss it. For that matter, no one in the family ever chose to make any inquiries. We just enjoyed it.

He would buy my mother the most elaborate and large heart-shaped, beribboned box of chocolates and present it ceremoniously (and, my mother always exclaimed, unexpectedly) before breakfast. Taped to the box would be a large card containing gushing sentiment. ("Blather," he called such greetings when he was the recipient.) He circled the price on the back, a gentle taunt and brag at the same time. (It was my mother's habit to cross out the cost markings on cards she sent.)

The three children received miniatures—boxes and greetings—and all received lavish (for him) expressions of affection and warmth.

Love, I may safely call it.

Then, ordinary breakfast, and off he went, most years, to work. The evening meal was taken at a restaurant. Further celebration. This prevailing festive mood was almost entirely his. We others were an audience at his performance. We were enchanted—"awed," seems more appropriate—by the volley of emotional babble.

Many years later, the temptation to explain such seemingly uncharacteristic behavior lingers. I have, by now, swallowed more ideas than I can digest. One is most palatable, at least.

The Romans, after all, conceived of Cupid as a mischievous boy who provoked both love and repulsion with his arrows. This casting was compatible with my father's type. Also, there is, and has been for quite some time, the theory that St. Valentine's commemoration—the feast day of February 14—actually came about by association with a pagan festival. This, and the correlative martyrdom, the saint's singularly and my father's annually, encourage a hauntingly happy hypothesis. (He was, you see, very well read.)

Ah well, the feelings I feel probably go beyond my genes, despite the fact that, in my own way, I seem to emulate my father.

I have been inspired by others' more creative celebration, though they may have been perfectly in keeping with their typical modes of behavior.

I find particularly inspiring the story of a Long Island housewife who opened her door to find a man dressed in shining armor. Indeed, it was her husband, who then took her into the Big Apple for dinner at a restaurant with medieval décor. He wore his armor and had a grand time, as did his lady-in-waiting.

A New Hampshire couple was picked up at La Guardia Airport and taken by limousine to a Manhattan hotel where they entered a suite lit by candles and filled with flowers, fresh fruit, cheeses, chilled champagne, heart-shaped balloons and chewing tobacco (for the gentleman). Operatic music was playing from a tape deck. A filmy blue peignoir rested tastefully on the bed. And a flower floated in the toilet bowl.

Somewhere my father smiles.

Yet, my own anticipatory excitement is somewhat dampened by the thought of all those who cannot share it. I remember, too well, the poet Herrick:

> Oft have I heard both youths and maidens say
> Birds choose their mates and couple, too, this day:
> But by their flight I never can divine
> When I shall couple with my Valentine.

To all the Herricks out there: I hope you find pleasure in poetry.

38

An Old Man and a Sand Castle

The Miami Herald, March 15, 1981

Anita, the kids and I traveled to Florida to visit my sisters during a spring break from school. One of my sisters lived right on the beach in Ft. Lauderdale. It was a wonderful visit. Except for one morning, a light-hearted, good time was had by all.

My son and I went down to the beach early that morning. Dan was fifteen at the time. He built a sophisticated sand castle—then frolicked in the sea—leaving me to observe and drift into worlds of thought that were in cadence with the incoming waves.

My son returned to his castle moments before an elderly gentleman strolled toward us.

I never came to Ft. Lauderdale beach as a college student—beer in hand, sun lotion in pockets, females in mind, life in tow. Many have; many still do. These collegiate conquistadors come to the ocean's edge confidently, with no definition of time, no particular respect for the sea's indifferent vastness and no concern for the personal tides that sweep over us, wash us clean and allow us our tomorrows.

And so would I have come to this Atlantic shore with all these irreverences—and with the additional intolerance toward old men's prattle. But being in my 40's now, being in the old age of youth, I have learned to make all sorts of allowances, particularly for the aged.

As it turned out, I didn't have to tolerate "prattle" on this particular February morning.

I stood, back to the seas, watching my son building the proverbial castle in the sand precariously close to the waterline. An old man distractedly walking past us stopped abruptly and stood gazing—silent until moments later, after the tide had had its inevitable way. My son began to build a new structure immediately.

The old man looked at me. "The young don't have futility in their vocabulary," he said in a pronounced Italian accent. A pause "Thank God," he added. Thus it began.

I don't ask strangers for oral autobiographies. But attentive eyes are enough, very often, to elicit personal tales. Especially woeful tales. I was annoyed at my eyes' provocativeness. Yet, I was to be affected. By substance and by style.

He lives in Toronto. He came from "the old country" 20-some-odd years ago; I don't know the exact figure, because I was listening to his voice, not his words at the time. He came to Florida to visit "a sick sister," he said, tapping his forehead with an index finger. "Getting sicker; too bad. I take her for walks on the beach, but first I come by myself while she's getting ready. That gets me ready. Know what I mean?"

His oldest son was 17 when the man and his wife left for Canada. "I didn't know anything but work, so we all worked. We worked with our bodies." He showed his work hands—more to himself than to his confidante.

The other sons, two of them, born in "the modern world," went to college. "The youngest one still does. He'll study the rest of his life, not to work."

The sons don't like each other. He doesn't like them. They don't like him. "Worse yet, they don't love me." He nodded toward my son. "He love you?" He didn't wait for the answer I wasn't going to give him.

His wife died a few years ago. She was the last person he had left who loved him and respected the past. "We came across that ocean." He faced the sea fully. "So sad, so fresh, the days that are no more," he recited.

"Tennyson," I said. He didn't hear. "Praise the sea, but keep the land," I said.

"Tell him, not me," he said, gesturing toward the castle builder. "Memories are all I've got now, and even them … You know poetry?" He didn't wait for the answer I was about to give him. "Joy's recollection is no longer joy; sorrow's memory is sorrow still."

"Byron," I said. He didn't hear.

"I used to tell my sons it's not what they have or what they do that says what they're worth, but what they *are*." He spit philosophically against the incoming tide, the gesture of a melancholy man, not an irate Italian. "I never dedicated my life to destiny," he said.

He turned back, looking away from the seas, looking at me, then at the tide-torn sand castle nearby. "You can't build on regrets; you can only drown in them. The young understand that," he said. "The old talk and think about things that don't matter at all. And the regrets take the place of dreams." His eyes began to tear.

"The old know too much," I said awkwardly. He didn't hear.

I looked at him carefully for the first time—at his tight, slight body. A plain white tee-shirt tucked into red bathing trunks. A clean-shaven face but for the impeccable gray Adolphe Menjou mustache. A face darkened more by life than by nature. A look that mocked the injustice of life's verdict.

Then, suddenly, a gap-toothed smile. A smile to dissipate the shadow cast by bone and bitterness. A smile that revealed that the best of everything felt or understood is never put into words.

He shook my hand and—without a word—departed. The surf roared in; another castle was swept away.

"Good luck!" I shouted after him.

He didn't hear—thank God.

39

Coffee Cutoff Causes Chaos

The Boston Herald American, April 23, 1981

More foolishness from officialdom. Vermont's Governor, Richard Snelling, sensitive to fiscal difficulties in his state, took the bull by the tail—and ended up with more than egg on his face. It was a story I had to jump on—and I did.

Yankee Magazine saw the story, and their cartoonist jumped also. I'll quote the cartoon's heading.

"Boston Herald American—According to an article by Harvey A. Dorfman, the governor of Vermont has cut off free coffee for the state legislators who came by his office each morning for conversation and planning—in order to save money."

The cartoon under this heading shows a speaker at a podium. The message delivered to his audience, the legislators, is wrapped in the cartoonist's bubble. The speaker's words: "...and the Governor tells me that his new policy has already, in just the first week, saved $12.38."

The lawmakers are all asleep at their desks—zzz's filling the room.

These are precious days and few for the Governor of the State of Vermont, who earlier in the legislative year made a considerable blunder. This blunder has been, to a great extent, responsible for a sleepy session of the General Assembly. Hundreds of proposals have been made; little action has been taken. The Governor must hope that he has enough tolerant and understanding friends in the state Capitol to forgive, if not forget—unless in the closing days he rectifies his egregious error.

What the Governor did—I'm certain readers this morning will grasp their cups with subconscious tenacity at the news—what the Governor did, I must report, was to curtail, halt, stop, cut off—there, that's it truly—cut off free coffee for the state legislators who often came by for coffee and conversation.

Four years ago, when the Governor was sworn in, he established a morning hour every day, during which time his State House door would be open to lawmakers. Coffee was served, of course, and the ritual gave the Governor an excellent opportunity to listen and to lobby. This year he pulled the plug on free coffee. The Governor is said to have had a sharp decline in morning visitors as a result of that decision. He is said to be unable to understand why. He is said to have pinched a petty penny.

There are still the final, most important days left before the 1981 General Assembly disassembles. The Governor is waiting anxiously for his recommendations to be acted upon. He has attempted, without success, to get his state aid to education formula properly redesigned. He hasn't gotten all the state troopers he asked for; he's failed to get fully funded highway and capital construction budgets, or his anti-crime bills, or a measure to promote tourism. Most significantly, his veto on a tax break for theaters was overridden. And so on. The legislators are still waiting for their coffee.

Some observers in Montpelier believe that the state administration has lost touch with the legislative body because of this circumstance. One legislative leader, who, of course, wished to remain anonymous (he's a Republican), felt that "one meetin' a week just weren't enough. And I'll tell ya, I don't fancy to walkin' around with this here thermos."

A number of other legislators were interviewed; similar views were expressed. The remainder were asleep and could not be roused, though the expressions on their faces were evidence enough of their attitudes.

But let us discuss coffee for a moment. Quite obviously, the Governor did not do much homework on the subject before acting to change his stance. Unfortunate. To begin with, coffee goes way back—farther, even, than Ethan Allen. It was discovered as a beverage in Ethiopia prior to the thirteenth century. An Arabian mullah saw his goats browsing on coffee leaves and berries. The animals then gamboled excitedly over the hillsides all through the night. The mullah gave an infusion to his monks hoping to keep them awake during their devotionals. It worked. That implication alone should have made itself apparent to the Governor.

Many populations served (and still do serve) coffee as a symbol of welcome and an encouragement for conversation. Message number two.

Just about 300 years ago Charles II of England closed 3,000 coffee houses. He knew where the action started. Charles rescinded his edict a few days later, under the pressure of public demand. These words to the wise are advice, not demand. It is common knowledge, or should be, that the coffee room in Washington, D.C. has been responsible for more revelation than the Congressional Record. Politicians, after all is said and done, live in the repute of the commonality, and where is that better felt (aside from stag parties) than within the caffeined cacophony of a free-coffee klatsch?

If the Governor truly believes his policy is saving money, he should remember that money, like manure, must be spread around to accomplish anything. Like manure, coffee accomplishes. It produces physiological and psychological effects. It stimulates; it is action-oriented. The drink expands the blood vessels so more blood flows to the heart and to the brain. Legislators sometimes use these parts. Hearts and brains are very helpful in conducting public affairs for public advantage. Such legislation is worth $2 a pound, I'd say.

Politics may be the science of exigencies to the Governor, but to me science always seems to open a door with more doors behind it. In other words, science never solves a problem without creating a bigger one. The bigger problem, in this case, is the Governor's lessened contact and compatibility with state senators and representatives. The Governor should know that the confidence of others is a politician's fulcrum, and though politicians are rarely expected to distinguish between right and wrong, they must nevertheless work as effectively as possible together for the people they represent.

Must the General Assembly work during these remaining days of the current sessions in the unseasonable and unreasonable chill which came on the icy gust of the Governor's pronouncement? Will there be no free coffee to warm our elected representatives to their 11th-hour tasks? There is still time for countermanding action on the Governor's part. The truest particle of power is duty. The message should be clear enough.

A warning: Hot chocolate is not a viable alternative. Jelly beans are plain silly. Vermonters will watch and wait.

Postscript—Vermonters—and legislators—didn't have to wait very long. Days after the article appeared (also in The Rutland Herald, *a state paper) the free coffee policy was reinstated.*

40

Pragmatism Is Perpendicular

The Rutland Herald, May 28, 1981

It never ends. Into my line of vision—from a newspaper clip—came another example of man's seemingly unlimited capacity for foolishness. Mark Twain said long ago that the difference between man and other animals is minimal "and most of time he forfeits the difference" (meaning his—our—brain).

Further proof, if you need it, is furnished below, with some regional condescension thrown in.

Rutland—Vermont has Calvin Coolidge; Iowa has Herbert Hoover. Vermont has cows; Iowa has hogs. Vermont has the mountains; Iowa has the flats. The differences are evident.

More significantly, Vermont has Rutland Postmaster Ken Yates; Iowa has Des Moines Postal Supervisor Darrel Mathews. Here, some further discussion is required.

A while back on those western flats of "The Hawkeye State," a fellow named Robert McLaughlin, an 11-year veteran of mail sorting, found himself suspended from his job and docked $100 or so in pay for holding letters at a 90-degree angle to his line of vision while sorting them.

Boss Mathews cited postal clerk McLaughlin for insubordination. The official letter read, in part: "You (McLaughlin) refused to hold your mail at a 45-degree angle as I have instructed you to do. You insisted that your method of holding was superior to the method I instructed you to employ."

Mr. McLaughlin wears bifocals.

Mr. Mathews lives too close to sea level for his own good.

Mr. McLaughlin challenged the suspension and said he was determined to "get rid of this personal harassment ... They haven't ever enforced this (rule) before, and, by God, if they did, it would really mess things up."

Mr. Mathews didn't respond.

The origins may be traced to a training session under the Postal Service's Manual Operations Methods Improvement Program, which Mr. McLaughlin said was designed to give "tips" to employees on how to sit on their stools and sort letters. A line drawing in the guidebook illustrates a right way—and a wrong way. The right way is to hold the letter at a 45-degree angle, "one foot on the floor at all times." The wrong way is any variation of the right way.

The booklet was written by someone living too far above sea level for anyone's good.

Power in the Des Moines post office is expressed in self-reverence, rather than in self-control. Such expression leads to tyranny. Authority should be the collective general sense of the wisest members of the department to which they belong. Such authority leads to West Street in Rutland, Vermont.

Ah, this sounds like saucy pride, indeed. But when the truth is ripe, it must be plucked.

So here in Rutland we meet the pragmatic Postmaster, Ken Yates, whose philosophy of mail sorting represents sapience at its simplest, and who said, "As long as the mail gets into the proper sort, I'm satisfied." Illustrating why simplicity is most profound.

Mr. Yates found no evidence of the 45-degree angle "rule" in a general *Craft Skill Training Manual* in his office. He did say that "movement costs time, and the less time lost, the better."

Mr. Yates then made an accompanied tour of the sorting area and elaborated on practical methodology. "All stamps must be down and to the right" when set on the ledge before the sorter and his cases. "No lefties can sort. All of it must be done right-handed. It's the only practical way."

Other practical approaches can be found in Yates' office manual. These are listed under "Coordinating Eyes and Hands."

Pick up a solid handful of mail with the left hand. Since the stamps are down and facing to the right, the mail will be in proper reading position when picked up.

Push the top letter slightly forward with the left thumb so that the right thumb and index finger can grasp the outer edge of letter. The left thumb serves as a feeder.

Read the (street) address only. Develop sight recognition of addresses as whole units (along the line). Recall the correct separation and place the letter on shelf at right or left side of separation to correspond with number.

As the letter is pushed fully into separation, position eyes on next letter and push next letter forward with left thumb. The right hand then returns to pick this letter for placing into the proper separation.

Follow the same procedure in the distribution of each letter, and coordination of eyes, hands, fingers and memory will improve until the process becomes automatic.

Automatic! And what if some unique, individual, but still "automatic" approach to sorting is utilized by a sorter—such as holding letters at a 90-degree angle? "If it helps the sorter to be more efficient, then it's OK with me," said Ken Yates.

Mr. Yates wears bifocals; Mr. Yates is a Vermonter.

Not to demean the state of Iowa entirely (though out there they still haven't changed the rules to allow girls to play basketball the way boys do), let it be noted that some historical credit is due. Iowa's first governor, Ansel Biggs (1846-1859), was born in Vermont. They've been in quest of a proper angle since his tenure ended.

41

Banana Belt Still Fights an Old Battle

The Rutland Herald, August 15, 1981

Having resigned after my four-year tenure as a girls' basketball coach, I was able to do more writing, which is what I had really wanted to do all along. Steve Terry, the managing editor of the Herald, *now had me doing feature stories, aside from the regular Thursday column and random sports pieces.*

I was interviewing state dignitaries and those who came to our state as vacationers or tourists. When left to my own devices, I tried to come up with ideas that were ignored by the other state papers.

Bennington Battle Day was soon to be celebrated in that town, just over the Massachusetts border, and the rival Banner *would fill its pages with schedules, human interest stories, historical retrospectives and the like.*

I suggested to Steve we run a piece about Bennington. His eyebrows rose. I told him I'd come at it from another point of view—a sympathetic piece—sort of—talking about how Bennington is a state step-sister. It's so far south, I reminded him, they still say it's in the 'banana belt.'

His less-than-enthusiastic response was, "What the hell; go ahead. We'll surprise the shit out of the Banner *for paying any attention at all." Then he issued a warning: "Don't be poking fun at the town; this is front page stuff, not your page." (He was referring to the Thursday section where my 'Miscellany' column appeared.) I assured him I would be discreet.*

As for my feelings about the completed article, well, Steve liked it, so that was OK. I thought it not very entertaining. He said articles like this aren't meant to entertain; they're meant to inform. (Oh, I knew that, but ...) So why did I include it in this volume? Probably because I was somewhat entertained after all by the northern folks I talked to on the phone; maybe the readers would be also.

Bennington—On August 18, 1777, a battle was won at Bennington that helped turn the tide in the war for American independence.

As the town celebrates the 204th anniversary of the event this weekend and next, Bennington still finds itself in a different kind of battle, against a more resistant tide, one which many local citizens believe washed over their town for too many years.

What has formed as a result, they believe, is a *terra incognita*—an unknown place—insofar as the rest of Vermont is concerned.

Many Benningtonians have already surrendered in the battle for statewide recognition. Their identity up north is obscure, at best; insignificant, at worst, they claim.

John Proud was a stock clerk in Adams' Clothing Store on Main Street as a boy. Today he owns the business. And he is convinced the northern part of the state more or less "owns" Vermont.

"They think the Indians are still around (here)," Proud said.

One of his young salesmen nearby added his own view that Bennington is considered a non-entity in the latitudes above the so-called "Banana Belt."

Proud believes this kind of segregation has political causes. "And they're a different breed of cat up there," he said. "Friendly enough, but distant."

Psychologically, as well as geographically, the haberdasher explained.

"I know this," said the proprietor of Beecher's Drug Store. "Bennington gets the raw end of anything (to do) with the highway."

Such were the general views that prevailed up and down Main Street.

But realtor T. Garry Buckley, who rubbed many northern elbows while serving his county as a member of the state Senate, offered a fuller explanation of Bennington's statewide identity crisis.

"We're actually in an evolutionary wind-down from that attitude toward Bennington," Buckley said. "Because the rest of the state is now more cosmopolitan itself."

Buckley believes the "Banana Belt reached its peak in the 50's." All manner of parochialism existed in those days, he claimed.

"Republicans couldn't lose in Bennington County; a Catholic couldn't win north of Arlington, south of Wallingford; a Republican Catholic was held suspect by everyone.

"But that all changed," Buckley declared. "The last vestige of (overt) prejudice disappeared. And Bennington started to develop a cohesion and a (good) reputation."

Buckley cited two major factors for Bennington's new image, such as it may be: the work of the Bennington Industrial Corp. ("mostly the efforts of the late Francis Morrissey") and the improvements to Route 7.

Another problem Bennington had to cope with was its own lack of organization.

"Actually," Buckley recalled, "there was the village of North Bennington, the village of Old Bennington, the village of Bennington—and the town. It was a jungle if you wanted to find your way around," Buckley said, "even if you were a local."

Again he attributed great change to Francis Morrissey. "He turned this into a fiery, proud little community. There were others, of course, like Charley Feinberg. They were catalysts. They brought new industry in after the woolen and textile mills left. Now we still have a wide variety of small industry. I'm sure the pride is still here," said Buckley.

His historical view of northern Vermont perceptions of this southern town seems to illustrate his own pride.

"It isn't that they felt superior to us," he said. "We felt superior to them. In the 50's there were more hicks in Rutland and Burlington than here. We had Bennington College; we had the industry; we were more cosmopolitan than the rest of the state."

Buckley continued, "I remember going to Golden Gloves boxing matches (upstate). The Bennington boy, no matter how he fought, had class. Tidy trunks, proper shoes. All the others looked like they came out of a barn.

"I used the term "Banana Belt' myself when I was in the Senate. It was an easy out for a politician. I used it for a laugh, but actually the northern people have been good to us. Much of what we sensed was part of our imagination," said Buckley.

Gloria Van Derzee, the executive director of the Bennington Chamber of Commerce, has devoted her imagination to building Bennington's reputation. The greatest results, however, have come from out of state.

Broad coverage has been given to Bennington by *The New York Times*, *The Boston Globe* and *The Hartford Courant*.

Also by an Albany television station. Television's "P.M. Magazine" will cover the re-enactment of the Battle of Bennington next week.

"People come to Bennington from New York, Massachusetts, Pennsylvania—all of New Jersey seems to be here during the summer," said Van Derzee. "Our town is known for its peaceful and bucolic atmosphere. And even more for its history. That monument is the true symbol of Bennington."

Though Bennington continues to popularize the Green Mountain Boys' exploits against John Burgoyne's Redcoats, Van Derzee believes the contemporary exploits of Bennington's craftsmen bring considerable crowds to the area.

August was proclaimed as Vermont Craft Month. "Not a tremendous amount of attention was paid to it, but Gov. Snelling came here to the Bennington Museum to begin it officially," said Van Derzee.

She is most proud of recent state funds granted to the Greater Bennington Chamber of Commerce. "We received $18,750," Van Derzee said. "We're the only town that received that much money from the travel division. It shows we're doing something significant to bring people into the area."

The fact remains, northern Vermont people stay away in droves.

A number of Vermonters were selected at random for brief telephone interviews. The prerequisite for selection was residency in Rutland or points north.

Stanley Kulic of Norton said, "I don't know nothing about Bennington. I've never been there. Always meant to go. Probably never will."

Ernest Barney of Montpelier, an elderly man who admits to being over 16, doesn't know "a helluva lot" about Bennington. "Why should I?" he asked. He doesn't remember if he's ever been there.

Mrs. Mario Ciardelli of Burlington knows she's never been to Bennington, but she said, "I've heard a lot about it."

Positive or negative?

"Negative."

What, specifically?

"Let me think. Maybe it was about Middlebury. I don't seem to know anything about Bennington," Mrs. Ciardelli decided.

Stephen Wood of St. Johnsbury thinks he knows only one thing. "Isn't there a Bennington Battle Day?" Wood has lived in Vermont all his life. His wife is from Bennington. "I don't think I'd even know how to get there," he said.

Susan Hollister has been to Bennington. She performed there, dancing. She thinks the town is a pretty one. Currently she lives in Hyde Park. She claims most of the people she knows think "everything south of Montpelier is in another state."

One Burlington woman thought Bennington was in Massachusetts.

Bennington is approximately 50 miles south of Rutland, where Peggy Ryan lives. She "know(s) very little about Bennington, to tell the truth."

Pinned down, she truthfully couldn't say anything she knew at all. "It's been 27 years since I went through there."

She didn't stop.

Many people will stop this weekend and next to join in the celebration of Bennington's historical and—yes—civic pride.

It is believed that few of these visitors, relatively, will arrive from the north. Benningtonians seem to have acclimated themselves to that circumstance. And many of them don't care that much if the upstaters ever come.

42

Galbraith's View of Vermont

The Rutland Herald, August 24, 1981

"He's an international figure who lives part time in Vermont," said the managing editor. "I'll get you through the door; the rest is up to you. I'll give you a bonus if you can make him smile. I'll trust you."

J.K. Galbraith was not a challenging interviewee; he was interested in the topic his interviewer had asked him to expand upon: the state of the state of Vermont, so to speak. His fondness for the state was very apparent.

Townshend—The very thing that attracts people to Vermont is what can destroy it, according to John Kenneth Galbraith, economist, teacher, critic, diplomat, advisor to presidents and frequent resident of this town.

In a recent interview, Galbraith, the Paul M. Warburg Professor Emeritus of Economics at Harvard University, said "the greatest danger Vermont faced 20 or 30 years ago—and still faces—was that its natural beauty would attract industry and commerce that would destroy it.

"The long-standing history of any attractive part of the country is that it attracts not only the people but the roadside commerce, the billboards, the signs, the filling stations and housing developments—all of which destroy the beauty. This is the essence of the tourist area. Nobody should doubt it," Galbraith said.

He believes that, on the whole, this has been recognized here, and that control of economic development has done a better job of "preserving the ambience" and beauty of Vermont "than in any other state in the union."

Galbraith cited New Hampshire as a contrasting example.

"One has only to cross the Connecticut (River) to see the billboards and random development and to see what a good job Vermont has done," he said.

Galbraith acknowledged that Vermont is a poor state, but he was firm in his view that it has not sacrificed economics for cosmetics.

"If the preservation movement had not been successful," he said, "Vermont's economy would have been much worse. No question. The great industry in this part of the world is residential—the attracting of people who find this an agreeable place to live. This has been one of the great developments of our time. The other thing has been (bringing about) the economic activity which is associated with an attractive neighborhood. This is one of the things that has saved Vermont and a few other states," Galbraith said.

"One of the consequences has been that we're not attracting old-fashioned manufacturing enterprises. One should applaud (this consequence)," Galbraith said.

The loss of those 'tedious, old industries," he said, can be associated with the improvement of income in New England. "When we let the textile industry go south, we did ourselves a major favor."

All the practical, down-to-earth men wept when these textile mills and the shoe factories left this part of the country, he said. He advised that we "always mistrust the wisdom of down-to-earth men," in this case those who wept over the loss of industries which kept their area poor.

A favorable future for Vermont is inextricably tied to the maintenance of the environment now, Galbraith believes.

He warned, "There's nothing more important. That's what brings the people with money to spend; that's what brings the kind of economic activity that pays good wages. Vermont is never going to be a rich state, but it's going to be far more affluent than (it would) if it let down the barriers of environment."

Vermont natives—"true Vermonters"—agree with this view, Galbraith believes. He claims they appreciate environmental aesthetics "even more than visitors."

Galbraith said he knows his Vermont neighbors very well. He told of one who says he never wakes up in the morning or retires at night without reflecting on his own happiness over the distant view of the Green Mountains and Hogback.

Vermont's contribution to the rest of the United States, Galbraith supposed, is "the visual opportunity for the rest of the country—those who come here to visit it."

But a greater contribution in America, Galbraith added, was in Vermont's having over the years—"ever since George Aiken—the smallest but most sensible congressional delegation in Washington. This is still true." he said.

"Jeffords was showing in his vote (as the lone opponent to President Reagan's tax bill) some Vermont independence," Galbraith said. "I couldn't help noticing up in Montpelier the other day, when I was at a meeting with him, that he got more applause than anybody else."

Galbraith felt Vermonters had a perception that the Reagan administration was "engaged in a giveaway program for the rich."

Galbraith also felt that Vermont has been a well-governed state. He had associations with former Govs. Philip H. Hoff and Thomas P. Salmon, but is not "close to Gov. Snelling," claiming it to be a matter of politics.

Galbraith's personal introduction to this state came in 1947, when he and his wife purchased his isolated Townshend acreage.

"I was away in Germany in 1945," he recalled, "when my wife came up here and lived for a summer with some friends in Brookline. She fell in love with Vermont, and the following year we instituted a search for a place of our own here.

"The process of searching was so pleasant—and there were so many extremely attractive places available for so little money—we eventually became worried that we'd keep on looking forever. Then one day we hit upon this. We decided that this (area) was not going to be overwhelmed by suburbia. The countryside around here has changed very little since we bought the place in August of 1947," Galbraith said.

Galbraith has never managed to develop a fondness for Vermont winters. He said they are "too black and white"—stark. And they remind him too much of his austere environment while growing up in Canada.

"Our general practice is to come here from late spring until the time Harvard starts in mid-September," he said. "There should be no question that the great months in Vermont are from July until the end of October."

One of Galbraith's justifications for coming here is his work—his writing. Always somewhat on the margin of public affairs and politics, he has "accumulated an enormous number of people" in Cambridge who make an equal number of claims on his time with their demands and requests.

"I don't do them," Galbraith said, "but I have to think up good excuses. When they hear I'm in Vermont, they say, 'Oh well, we mustn't trouble him.' So I have much more uninterrupted writing time here than when I'm at home. And for that reason, I have perhaps deserted Cambridge more than I should over a lifetime," he said.

Some people, however, are particularly anxious to see him when he is in Vermont. For example, within the past two weeks Galbraith has been interviewed by television crews from Japan, Sweden, France and Holland. An Italian crew was two days late at the time of this interview.

"They are all delighted for the chance to come to Vermont. They consider that an ideal background for a television interview in order to hear my somewhat somber views of the Reagan administration," said Galbraith.

Galbraith persuaded himself that by coming to Vermont he improves the quality of his work. "I doubt that anybody else can see that," he said. "But we all have our rationalizations."

Galbraith does extend himself beyond the limitations of his land's borders. He involves himself in state and community projects. Currently, his efforts are being extended in behalf of Marlboro College and its music festival.

"I would encourage all Vermonters to help in assuring the continuance of both," Galbraith said.

Personally speaking, Galbraith wishes—instead of retiring—"to write a novel." (He wrote a three-month best-seller approximately 10 years ago entitled *The Triumph*. His memoir, *A Life in Our Time,* was published in May.)

"The happiest years of my life were when I was doing that before, and I am going back and do another novel," he said.

Asked what he would like to see happen in America right now, Galbraith responded, "I'd be glad to see that people discovered that the future is not with the privileged. How's that?"

Postscript—After having looked the article over, Steve Terry puffed out his cheeks, pursed his lips, bobbed his head like a chicken pecking at feed and told me he was "pleased."

I informed him that I'd made Galbraith laugh. "How did you manage that?" he asked. "By doing an imitation of you."

He picked up the tab when we next went to eat at the Chinese restaurant across the street from the office—where staff members regularly met to dine and deliberate.

John Kenneth Galbraith died in 2006 in Cambridge, Massachusetts, of natural causes. He was 97 years old.

43

Herbie Dorfson Fights Back

The Hartford Courant, November 3, 1981
(Also run by *The Rutland Herald*)

Another wonderful (read: harebrained) bureaucratic idea. The folks who ran out of pen-cils to sharpen in Washington's policy-making rooms came up with a good one. I had read about it in the paper and seen a clip of a talking head on TV.

New York metropolitan area folks were disturbed by the thought of the possible conse-quences of a nuclear attack or some other outrage perpetrated on City man—Metropoli-tan Area Man included—by Other man.

Was this just water cooler chat? Wherever the plan was conceived, it was real—and this was the gist of it: families from Connecticut, New York City and Westchester County would be evacuated if such a circumstance developed. They would flee from their homes to seek safe havens elsewhere. Where? Well beyond the threatened or afflicted area. Say Vermont?

Yes, Vermont (and other outlying states in the Northeast). Each family would be 'put up' with a family in, say, Vermont. Protected, sheltered, and fed. Embraced? Yes, that would be the solution. For those folks.

Living in a ski resort area, I had some trepidation. My experience with the breed— weekend skiers—at local markets, post office and restaurants conjured up what Shakespeare called "horrible imaginings." My son, a high-schooler who worked weekends at Bromley, one of the three ski mountains in our immediate area, fed my bias with 'ski-bunny' stories based on his own experiences. Stories of people whose social sensitivity is pre-empted by a sense of entitlement. Hosting (for an undetermined length of time) such interlopers would be demanding, inconvenient and generally unpleasant. Selfish attitude? Yes.

I was agonized by my bias. So I purged myself with this piece—a response to an upset-ting conceptual event presented as an imagined telephone conversation with a potential refugee-guest.

The ringing sounded at 11:14 p.m., according to my bedside digital clock, so the time was actually 11:12. I was startled out of a deep sleep; I numbly reached for the phone.

Hello?

Dorfson?

Dorfman!

Yes, Dorfman.

Speaking.

Charlie Wilpern here.

Who?

Charles Wilpern, Ridgefield, Connecticut. My boy. If you're Herbie …

Harvey!

Yes, Harvey Dorfson … Dorfman, that is. Then I've got the right party.

There's no party here, and you've disturbed a pretty fine sleep, as a matter of fact. Who the dickens are you, and what do you want at this hour?

Early to bed, early to rise, eh? Smart boy. How old are you, son?

Forty-five.

Well … you sound like a child. Young spirit, I mean. The point is, Herbie, I've drawn your name from the Wartime Crisis Relocation Plan Lottery here in Connecticut.

What are you talking about, Mr. Wilpern?

Charlie, Herb. You mean you didn't get the word yet?

Apparently not. Did I win something?

Yes. Me and my family! Ha, ha. Don't you read the newspapers, boy? Hold on, I'll read you the clipping I've got. (Pause) I'm here, OK … "The Civil Defense Authority in Washington has arranged for 53,000 Connecticut residents to relocate to Bennington County, Vermont, should American leaders decide a nuclear attack is imminent. These people would join the 33,000 people who currently live in the county. The Connecticut residents would be asked to bring as many provisions as they would have room for in their cars and drive north on Route 7 to pre-designated towns in Vermont …" Say, Herbie, wouldn't 81 north to Brattleboro and over the mountain on 30 be better? We'd beat the traffic and miss all those damn tourist traps. (Pause) Herb, are you there?

Yes.

How many people in your burg, just for the helluvit?

A little over 3,000, I think.

You in control, Herb? You sound like an anchor under ice.

I'm OK … How many people are there in Ridgefield?

Oh, 20,000, give or take a gross. We'll be like prisoners in a pit, as the Bible says. I think it's the Bible. Anyhow, Herbie, I'm actually calling now to ask a few questions and advise you of a few things, so we can be doomsday operational, as they say. First, the business about provisions: don't count on much. Babs has six kids. Babs and I, that is, and not all that much trunk space, what with ski boots and clothes and the kids' games.

Did you say …

Second, no kapok pillows. Babs's really got an allergic condition. Mostly emotional, I'd say, but whatever … Third, well, still second really, no animals. There won't be room for them … and it's survival of the fittest in Schaefer City, heh, heh. Back to basics, you know. Please, no pets. Not only is Babs allergic, but she's scared stiff of them. We had to give Wally's turtle a burial at sea … flush, flush … because Babs couldn't stand the way the thing pretended to have no head. Well now, do you have anything to say, Herb?

How long does the plan have you staying here?

Good question. The pamphlet I've got says … wait a minute here … says, and I quote … "it would depend on the circumstances. If the attack were very close by and the fallout was extensive, Connecticut citizens would be forced to stay in Vermont for an extended period of time." End quote.

CONNECTICUT citizens would be *forced* …?

Now, now, Herbert. Do I hear that icy anchor in your voice? Listen up, young fellow: However degraded or wretched a fellow mortal may be, he is still a member of our common species. Who said that, do you know?

Ava Gardner to Mickey Rooney.

Very funny, Herb, but not quite right. The point is, you don't have to put on airs for us. Humility is the base of every virtue, you know. Consider yourself a brother of mine. By the way, how many bathrooms do you have up there?

None.

None!? What are you talking about, Herb?

We have an outhouse; a two-seater, luckily, but no indoor plumbing.

Electricity?

Sorry.

By gawk, that means your bath towels are hung out on clotheslines. Aaagh, that feels like number five sandpaper after a shower.

No shower.

I guess you don't subscribe to Forbes Magazine. I'd have to send a change of address notice ... Listen, Herb, which is the closest ski area to you?

What makes you so certain doomsday in Connecticut will come during the ski season?

I'm not thinking doomsday at the moment, Herb. I thought I ought to drive up with the family next winter and have a week or so practice run ... to make sure conditions would be go, if necessary. Satisfactory, that is. For all of us, of course. For the Wilperns and for the Dorfsons. Then, if we didn't think we could have a proper handle on the set-up, Babs and I could check a few real estate listings ...

But don't you *have* to stay with us? Isn't the plan organized using that premise?

Why, that's mighty brotherly of you, Herb, but in business school we were taught that there's a way to reorganize everything. If worse came to worse, we'd sneak off to our chalet in Readsboro.

You mean you own a chalet in Vermont, but still ...

Well, you see, our friends in Wilton, Connecticut, were assigned to Readsboro, so we rented our chalet to them, so they wouldn't have to put up with cramped quarters.

They don't have any children. They prefer privacy to intimacy. It takes all kinds to make a world, Herb… (Pause) Wait a minute, Herb. (Pause) Babs wants to know if you like disco. She's wild. But listen, Herb, don't worry about anything. You'll be able to use the whole deal as a really solid tax write-off, sonny boy. Get your act straightened out up there and we'll see you when the snow flies … Please God, not before. By the way, we'll have room for a few dozen hard rolls and some jelly doughnuts the way they're supposed to be made. Now get back to sleep, Herbo. I'll keep in touch.

Postscript: Order marches with measured strides; disorder is always in a hurry. As is the case with many spontaneous, hasty plans—this one was never implemented.

44

Lola Aiken:
Another View from Putney

The Rutland Herald, February 2, 1982

My managing editor—my boss—Steve Terry, had worked for George D. Aiken in Washington, D.C. on his legislative staff. Much of his responsibility was in public relations, writing papers and things like that. Steve loved Aiken, as did most Vermonters. But his knowledge of the man was much deeper than what others knew of Aiken.

One day Steve asked me to go over to see Aiken, by then retired, and interview him for the Herald. *Having heard so much about George Aiken, I was happy to take on the assignment, which went well. The 'Governor' (as he was always called in Vermont) and I hit it off.*

Some time later he suggested to Steve that I be sent over to his home in Putney again—this time to interview his wife, Lola. Steve was excited. I was neutral, at best. But I went—and became a great fan of Lola Pierotta Aiken, a woman who I would not attach to her husband if I had seen them standing at opposite ends of the room at a cocktail party. But they were very much attached. And though with a thinner thread, surely, I became bound to them.

Putney—She didn't vote for Ronald Reagan: she's a bit "scared" of him, but she thinks "he's going the right way." She thinks most wives are a lot smarter than their husbands ever give them credit for being. The politician she most admired—with the exception of her husband—was Mike Mansfield. She is an advocate of Gov. Richard Snelling.

She is Lola Pierotti Aiken, administrative assistant (34 years) to and wife (15 years) of former Sen. George D. Aiken.

Mrs. Aiken, contrary to reports published over the years, does have her own opinions and is willing—has been willing—to reveal them publicly.

In a recent interview, she allowed that it was less a reluctance on her part to speak out than a benign neglect on the part of others.

"Actually," she said, "Nobody ever asked me anything. They just went on the assumption I'd agree with everything the governor (Mr. Aiken) said. They were acting as if I didn't have an opinion of my own. They are wrong."

Mrs. Aiken, a Montpelier native, admits to having been a conservative influence on her more liberal husband. ("I was a radical," she said.) Her conservative views she attributes to her background. "My mother and father came as immigrants from Italy."

But Mrs. Aiken disdains political labels. "I feel deeply that people who need help should be helped," she said. "That's not being conservative. Barry Goldwater was considered such a damn conservative, but when somebody needed help that's where they went. They didn't go to someone like Sen. (Hubert) Humphrey for some reason. He was a liberal, though."

George Aiken sponsored the food stamp plan and Lola Aiken supported it. "I thought it was going to help primarily older people who really couldn't make it on what they had to do with. But I lost all my enthusiasm for it when young people started using it promiscuously," she said.

"You go into Grand Union and you see some girl (using food stamps) that you know should be out working, and then she gets into a car with a young fellow—a new car. That makes me mad.," Mrs. Aiken said.

The problem, she believes, is not in the program but in "whoever is administering it." She feels such matters can better be handled at local levels.

"I still believe in food stamps, but it should be monitored closely," she said.

Lola Aiken has monitored the political scene closely since going to Washington, D.C., as a staffer for George Aiken in 1941. She had, before that, worked in the Secretary of State's office in Montpelier when George Aiken was the governor.

"Well, the first year in Washington was a disaster. It takes so long to learn your way around. But once past that, it started clicking. And it was a small staff at that time, four or five people in each office," she recalled.

"They tell me today there are an awful lot of ambitious people around who are stepping on everybody's toes to get to the top. Power. In those days it was 'clerk' and 'assistant clerk.' Now you have 'administrative assistant,' 'case assistant,' 'executive assistant'—and everybody tries to figure out who's most important. Titles now mean so much," she said.

And efficiency now is not properly proportionate to the size of the staff, Mrs. Aiken claims.

"For instance, white papers. I asked a woman in a senator's office what she did. 'Oh, I wrote a white paper.' She gave me the subject. She was considered the expert," said Mrs. Aiken, who finds it hard to believe that a worker knows more about a subject than the boss. She believes it doesn't have to be so—even in these times. But, she feels, there are too many politicians too busy "maneuvering for power too."

Asked to identify a current U.S. Senator who is doing things 'her way,' Mrs. Aiken named Russell Long (D. La.). "I bet Russell knows what's going on everywhere. He's a man of great power, but the man on top must know what's going on."

Asked to assess the political scene closer to home, Mrs. Aiken said: "I think the state of Vermont is very fortunate. I think it has some really outstanding public officials. I'm a great booster of Dick Snelling; I think he's been one of our good governors—in a very tough time. He is outstanding, and sometimes people don't look at what he's doing because they get upset about what they consider brashness.

"And I think we've got some great people in the Legislature. I get a kick out of Peter Giuliani (R–Montpelier). I think we're fortunate to have someone who argues the way he does about things. You've got to have different opinions," she said.

"Jim Jeffords is doing an awfully good job. There may be things I disagree with him about, but his heart is in the right place," she said. So is his neck, which he sticks out on issues and which she likes, said Mrs. Aiken.

"He also gets around the state to see people, the way the governor did. That's the way to be informed—and loved. I think Vermont is a state in which politicians can still do that."

Not all bodes well for Vermont's political future, according to Mrs. Aiken. The growing size of staffs "troubles" her, primarily because she believes that more people will have to find more work to do—and more work will produce more waste—such as extraneous memos. "Memos only express the viewpoint of the staff person," she said. "I hear them talk about 'the volume of work,' but they generate a lot of their own work, which is unnecessary."

Newsletters are her particular target. "A campaign gimmick," she called them. "Do you realize how expensive those are? Not only are they expensive sending, but a lot of them come back, and you have to pay postage on it when it's returned. And this business of 'I co-sponsored this,' or 'I did that'—I don't like it, because you're trying to project that you're doing a lot, whether you are or not," she said.

"People wrote to the Governor," she said. "They got an answer immediately." (Mrs. Aiken always refers to Sen. Aiken as 'Governor,' a reference to Aiken's four years as governor, from 1937 to 1941.)

She believes that, by and large, public officials are really better than the public deserves, "for the amount of time we (the public) put into doing our share."

Lola Aiken has one pet hope which she feels will never become a reality. "I don't like long legislative sessions," she said. "It seems everything can be streamlined. What really bothers me is that we spend so much time introducing bills that we never go back and look at some of the laws we passed to see whether they're still good, whether they're working. We never eliminate anything."

So years ago, she suggested a moratorium to Mike Mansfield. She told him she'd like to see one congressional session devoted to "looking back and seeing what's been done, seeing if we're duplicating what we've got, eliminating it, then straightening it out in the next session." The appropriations would be kept going during that session, of course, but pragmatic scrutiny of past legislation would be the primary focus.

"It will never happen," she said. "You know why? I don't think enough headlines are made for politicians on anything like that."

Still, Mrs. Aiken reiterated her view that the people are responsible. "Politicians only do what the people that elect them want them to do, and they get the message fast if people don't like it. I go back and blame the people; I don't blame the politicians," she said.

Mrs. Aiken expressed a wide range of other views, on subjects such as New York's Mayor, Edward Koch ("I like him!"); redistricting in Vermont ("It bothers me; I can see why they had to do it, but I don't like it."); too few people involved in politics ("Political science professors and teachers should be harping on that more."); and Ronald Reagan ("I was for Bush, but I honestly believe that no one but Reagan could have shifted gears the way he has—and gotten away with it. I think they [Reagan administration] should all shut up; they talk too much. But I think '82 is going to be a good year—in spite of them").

Mrs. Aiken claimed to have "learned an awful lot" from Mr. Aiken. She was asked if he had learned anything from her. "I don't know, and he'll never tell," she said.

Someone once asked her, "Lola, how come you haven't run for the governor's seat?"

Mrs. Aiken responded, "Because I'd last 24 hours. I'd call it like it is—and I'd probably get shoved out pretty damn fast."

But Lola Aiken is happy with what she and her husband have accomplished together. "Working for Vermont was fun," she said.

As for her opportunity to express some of her views publicly, she said, "The Governor will probably give me hell now."

("That would be suicide," he said in the background.)

45

The Right Idea,
The Wrong Button

The Rutland Herald, April 1, 1982

It has been 28 years since I wrote the words below. E-mail, texting, tweeting, facebooking: good grief. I couldn't write a thing about all that, since it's as remote to me as the former planet, Pluto. Times change; my technological inclinations and capabilities remain the same.

I remember being told about the "complex machinery" of government when I was a boy. In those days, the reference was to partisan politics, vested interests, graft and good-old-fashioned wrong-headedness.

Today, the machinery is truly complex and more truly machinery. Wrong-headedness has become egregious error.

Error is a hardy plant, and its early flowering within the walls of the House of Representatives in Washington gives cause for great concern on this, the first day of April.

It seems Vermont's Rep. James Jeffords discovered earlier this week that he mistakenly voted against a measure he had meant to support.

"I guess the only explanation is that I pressed the wrong button," Jeffords said.

That's right, button. Giving credit where credit is due, an effective politician certainly knows the difference between "aye" and "nay," Republican and Democrat, chocolate and vanilla and a number of other things. But being an effective technocrat has also become one of his responsibilities. An ability to be very discriminating in his selection of the proper button is a prerequisite for casting a vote through the House's electronic system. That's right, electronic voting system.

"What can I say? I goofed," explained Jeffords. He said it was his first one in eight years in the House.

The measure itself was a non-binding resolution that Congress support federal insurance of savings accounts. Jeffords voted against it on March 18, after having voiced his support to banking groups the day before.

149

Mark Kaplan, D-Chittenden, who is expected to formally launch his House campaign next month, identified Jeffords' vote as a disservice to Vermont.

No one should be upset by Kaplan's good-old-fashioned political behavior. It is safe, if saucy; it is comedic, if calculating. Most importantly, it is human.

Voting by pushing a button is not.

Does such technology make government more exciting? Perhaps. More efficient? Perhaps not.

Some people think the most decisive changes modern technics have brought about are the changes in both our concepts and experience of space, time and energy. What the inventions of Leonardo anticipated and the gang of later inventors realized were devices for saving time, for shrinking space, for speeding motion and, as Lewis Mumford has written, "for accelerating natural processes."

Natural processes! Such as saying "Aye" or "Nay."

The faster we move, the less we see along the way. The quicker we communicate, the less we understand.

The automobile is capable of going very fast, but cars crawl along the streets of every major and most minor cities. Too much technical advance has brought frustration, social conflict—and the magnified mistake.

Jim Jeffords said a few of his congressional colleagues have made the same mistake he just made, but they blamed it on the computer.

"I don't think I'll try to do that," he said.

Admission is a fault half mended—almost.

At any rate, technology hasn't exactly whooshed us down the path to perdition. It has merely run over us as we've squatted by the side of the road scratching our heads, wondering which way our fleeting humanness has gone.

Ever the optimist, I can only hope that the next great world conflict will be settled through Atari warfare. Some buttons are less menacing than others; some mistakes are irrevocable.

That's no April Fool's joke.

46

It's Also the Molly Stark Trail

The Rutland Herald, April 25, 1982

"Vermont's Route 9 might well qualify as an appropriate parallel for Vermont poet Robert Frost's famous 'Road Not Taken'—if travelers between Bennington and Brattleboro had their way. They don't."

That was my opening for a piece about the state's infamous east-west passageway across southern Vermont. I did a companion piece—a side-bar—about the road as it used to be in, as Gov. George Aiken wrote in a note to me, "the good old days."

I chose it for inclusion instead of the main article for the sake of interest (mine) and length (much shorter).

Marlboro, Vt.—When folks in this area are speaking realistically, they call the main road going through here Route 9. When they speak disdainfully, they invoke a variety of epithets. But when they speak with reverential nostalgia, they call it the Molly Stark Trail.

Molly Stark, one should know, was the wife of General John Stark, who defeated the British at the Battle of Bennington. There was no Vermont then; this area was called The Hampshire Grants. Mrs. Stark was in the area of what is now New Boston, N.H. when her husband, quite westward, realized that the Hessians and the British might be more than he and his men could handle. He sent a courier east to fetch Molly, telling her to bring every able-bodied person who could shoulder a gun to Bennington.

The courier traveled the ground which became Route 9 and returned by the same path with Molly Stark and a motley band of settlers, woodsmen and trappers—actually anyone who could fire a gun—to bolster Gen. Stark's army.

"It was probably just a wilderness path that followed the stream," explained Arnold White, who was born on Hogback Mountain and whose family runs the Skyway Restaurant and gift shop there.

Stark defeated the British, but another sort of battle along this trail still goes on. It is a battle to gain funds for improvement of the road and, at the same time, not allow these changes to alter its scenic and historic character.

In 1978, an angry group of residents here turned out to resist plans of the Vermont Transportation Board to change Route 9 where it bypassed Marlboro Village.

Arnold White was particularly angry. Ronald E.W. Crisman, Transportation Agency secretary at the time, reminded people that area legislators had said Route 9 improvement was their first wish.

It still is, according to White. "You need a hernia belt on this road," White said. "It's a good place to take an enemy for a drive. I'd like to take off the bad corners, have some passing lanes added, straighten out dangerous curves—and dig a respectable base. We've got to have a new road bed. But we must keep the road's character. That's what the hell Vermont is all about," said White.

"There's not another road that has the views this one does," he said. "You can see Massachusetts, New Hampshire and Connecticut from here. The road was built for these views and for visitors. And named to create a historic image. It was changed during the 30's for scenic reasons. Thousands and thousands of people travel this road for that reason," said White.

He believes truckers and unions will bring pressure to bear for construction of a "speedway." Just the day before, White pointed out, a Grand Union truck, "speeding all the way over from Albany," hit a frost heave and knocked out the vehicle's underparts. A common occurrence, according to the Wilmington police chief's secretary, who claimed that car parts can often be found along the road. (She advocates reducing the speed limit from 50 to 25 m.p.h.)

"We want to continue to show off our beautiful state," said White. "It's as beautiful now as when my father bought this land on Hogback in 1922."

That was the year Arnold White was born, though the Molly Stark Trail hadn't been so named yet. And that was the year Wallace Nutting, in his book, *Vermont Beautiful*, wrote, "In most of our states it is dangerous to leave the main roads. In Vermont, however, the roads are so good one may often follow heavy grades over the highest hills, over narrow winding passes, without a jolt or a jar."

Today, the proprietress of Marlboro County Enterprises, a tourist gift shop, will tell you, with no pun intended, "The frost heaves make you sick to your stomach" on jolting, jarring Route 9.

Postscript—I had written a note to that fine gentleman, statesman and native Vermonter, former Gov. George D. Aiken, asking him if he had anything to say about the Molly Stark Trail/Route 9. (We had made each other's acquaintance when I did an article about him; we had become friends when I did an article about his wife.)

This was his response:

Dear Harvey,

*Let me tell you how proud I was when I came
up Woodford Mountain in my Model T in high
speed. May I also say that I have slept beside
Woodford City Pond (now Woodford Lake) in
order to go fishing. Also, I have fished through
the Moss Island for bullheads in the middle of
the day and I have dug hundreds of small maple
trees in Halifax.*

Route 9 was one of my favorite routes in the good old days.

47

Hell Hath No Fury
Like Nancy Kissinger

The Rutland Herald, June 17, 1982

One of the current sports clichés that swirls around in the world of babble just happens to appeal to me. Well, the concept does, at least. I am an advocate of the philosophy it represents. The words, "I've got your back," (as opposed to the attitude at the other end of the behavioral continuum which has one person throwing another "under the bus") suggest loyalty and overt support of someone or something we value.

A timely newspaper article related to this topic crossed my desk and an Abbott and Costello exchange with a friend (because of another sports cliché expressed by me) got me thinking. I couldn't resist expressing the thoughts below.

Dorset, Vt.—It was late autumn up near the Merck Forest in Rupert when and where I mouthed the old sports cliché about any competitive event that ends in a tie. "It's like kissing your sister," I said to a distracted, very non-jock-type friend of mine.

"Kissinger's sister?" he asked, puzzled completely. "I didn't even know Henry Kissinger had a sister." And he certainly didn't understand my analogy, he said, after an extended attempt at clarification.

"You don't understand my diction," I said, frustrated but laughing.

I have not taken the time to find out whether or not the former Secretary of State does, in fact, have a sister. But I can report that Henry A. Kissinger has an oak of a woman—a sheltering oak—in Nancy, his wife.

Apparently, a Newark, N.J., judge shares my admiration. Somewhat, at least.

Here's the story. Four months ago, Henry A. and Nancy were walking through Newark International Airport when they were spotted by a woman who happened to be distributing pro-nuclear literature. Distracted from her efforts, she turned her creative and vocal energies quickly to the distraction: Henry A. Kissinger. The woman shouted, swore, insulted him.

Here permit me to interrupt the story to state clearly and directly a personal philosophy of mine: one must attempt to maintain dignity—whenever possible.

Back to the story. Nancy Kissinger didn't find it possible to maintain dignity—and I'm glad for her and for the neck she choked. Well, the judge in Newark ruled last week that Nancy was not guilty of choking—that is to say, not guilty of trying "to harm the other woman." The judge said Nancy grabbed the woman's throat because she was concerned at the time for her husband's heart condition, and he judged Nancy's reaction to the other woman's outburst to have been "spontaneous, somewhat human."

I'm glad for the judge also. It was a somewhat sensible ruling.

Dignity be damned sometimes; loyalty be lauded; self-defense be sanctioned. In an age in which the best we often hope for is faint neutrality, Nancy's brand of somewhat humanness should be somehow honored. We can't all roll over and play dead when confronted or affronted or abused.

Dignity, says the big red book at my elbow, is "the presence of poise and self-respect in one's deportment..." and so on. Sometimes poise and self-respect don't swim in the same pond, however.

I've lost my poise, but managed to keep my self-respect. So have you, dear reader. We're all somewhat human from time to time. And at those times, if it feels right, it feels good. I remember losing my poise a couple of years ago when my daughter was trying to learn the technique of driving a car. She performed the correct maneuver while motoring along Route 30 through Dorset Village, but a boorish woman had her own views and screamed them—through open windows—into our car, through the otherwise calm air of a pleasant day.

The judge in Newark would have found my response very spontaneous and definitely human. The woman's throat was not affected, but her eyes and ears were—and her sensibilities, assuming she possessed any. And I'm sure the judge would acknowledge that my daughter's heart and her faith in the Department of Motor Vehicles Driver's Manual were my primary concerns. If he were also to judge that I lost some dignity in the process, I would concur. But that would be small enough price to pay.

A month ago, I was shouted at by a puff of a man, apparently inflated by his sense of self-importance. I offered my own sense of self in return, but he obviously thought it was insufficient. The situation deteriorated rapidly. His neck was in danger, I must admit. But he stalked off in time for a particle of my dignity to be retained. The possession of it made me feel terrible. I wished I had lost it all, but my son—a witness—assured me what was left wasn't worth mentioning. And he said I had made my point. (He's too sensible.)

One of my old friends seems to me to be more inherently dignified than I could ever possibly be. He's also calmer, gentler, more peace-loving—bordering on being a coward, he claims. But he was provoked enough to ask thrice, tell twice and threaten once the teenage boys who were annoying him and insulting his wife, through words and antics, as they all sat in a New York movie theater.

Luckily for him, his emotions had progressed to a point at which his threat seemed as credible to the nuisances as it was vulgar to his wife. The boys fled the wrath of the middle-aged bank executive. More than dignity might have been lost in that scenario. His wife still can't believe it was her man. Her heart is now in better condition than ever.

And there is the classic story of the Quaker who, though non-violent, was nevertheless irked beyond dignity and dogma. He fingered his musket and told the agitator across from him, "I would not harm thee for the world, brother, but thou stand'st where I shoot."

The idea that dignity must be maintained at all costs is an illusion that tries to save us pain and allow us to enjoy an easy pleasure instead. But Freud, I think, warned that our illusions are bound to collide with reality occasionally. When they do, these illusions are smashed to pieces—spontaneously—and we must accept the result without complaint.

Sometimes, we may even be able to muster a smile. I bet Nancy Kissinger smiled last week, I hope so.

I bet the other lady found the verdict hard to swallow. Serves her neck right. And does my heart good.

And that's better than kissing Henry Kissinger's sister.

48

Dad and Me

The Rutland Herald, June 20, 1982

I was asked to do a Father's Day piece. "Any slant—funny or whatever comes to your mind." Well, my father is always on my mind. By 1982, his ephemeral self had been gone for 25 years. So it was a sort of anniversary, and that provoked me to delve a bit deeper into a subject that, as I suggested, was always near the top of my consciousness. I hadn't written about him much, as I say in the piece. Might as well give it a go now, I thought at the time. Especially since it was 'by request.'

(I have since referred to him regularly in the anecdotal memoir 'trilogy' I wrote. Very regularly.)

My father died at the age of 62, a month before I graduated from college. That was 25 years ago. Since then, I've come to think that it may be true that when you lose a parent, you lose your past. Not necessarily all your past though.

Whatever the case, I'm moved in the present to make some sort of Father's Day commemorations and these words are it. Necessarily it.

Many such words have passed along, among and through the strata of my consciousness during this fatherless quarter century, but these are the first I have so purposely set down in print since my 1953 essay about the man, a part of the New York State High School English Regents Examination. My English teacher informed me that I had received all possible 30 points for that essay, though I don't recall one thing I wrote about my father. I know I never told him about my grand score or my aggrandized treatment of the subject.

I loved my father. I still do, though I don't recall ever having told him about that love when he was alive. And I know he never told me of his in so many words. Any words, really, that I can remember. Looks, gestures, subtle actions, yes. But I don't recall specific ones.

He was 40 when I, his only son, was born. Two daughters had been born 16 and 11 years prior to my birth. I was a rather sickly son during my first 12 years, but I don't recall displeasing or pleasing my father in any particular way. If I did, he didn't show it.

He gave me Darrow and Lincoln and Sholem Asch to read. He taught me to revere Mel Ott's New York Giants and disdain anyone's New York Yankees. He didn't tell me there was a God; he didn't tell me there wasn't one. He introduced me to the concept of a two-horse parlay and a three-horse round robin. He said many things I can't remember and some that I can. Like, "Suffering is the surest means of making us truthful to ourselves." I don't know if he was suffering at the time, or if he thought I was.

He was on a destroyer during World War I—the U.S.S. Bagley, I recall. He believed in Woodrow Wilson. I don't know if he believed in me. I hope he believed in himself. Sometimes I wonder.

To hear my sisters tell it, they and everybody else believed in him: his wife, his brother, his sisters, his many associates and few real friends. He had a special presence; I know that, though I never got the opportunity to truly define it.

I recall challenging it once. I was just about at the end of my debilitation and the beginning of my robustness. I was 13 and I responded disrespectfully to a command he had made, though I recall neither the substance of his words nor my response. But his after-remarks are still knit tightly in my sensibility, soft as they were in the original raveling: "Don't ever speak to me like that again, unless you think you can back it up." I recall the feeling of dying cells in me.

A year later, the initial scene was replayed. I was bigger and more often healthy. "Do you remember what I told you last year?" he said after my haughty rudeness.

I nodded my adolescent head in arrogant affirmation. He then told me to get down from the closet the two pair of 16-ounce English boxing gloves kept there. He followed me into the bedroom and waited silently as I reached for the gloves. I handed them to him. He put one pair on my hands then tied the laces. He slipped his hands loosely into his gloves. We faced each other in the middle of the floor. I recall my rended self, feeling first what I now know to have been the desire every son has, in some way, to slay his father; feeling foremost what I then knew was overwhelming desire to embrace him and ask, if not beg, forgiveness.

Pride spoke louder than love. I threw what I thought to have been a crisp left jab, as he had taught me after my having absorbed a street drubbing years before. I knew what hit me, though I don't recall ever having seen it come. I was propelled backward; I slammed into an old rickety chair, topped it, banging my head on the apartment-house steam pipe and slid to the floor feeling heat behind and within me, feeling ice hovering over me in my father's face, frozen by disgust. I recall thinking it was disgust with me, though I now know it was disgust with himself.

My father could throw a rubber ball—behind his back—from the street onto a six-story apartment building roof. He couldn't very well throw an arm around a son's shoulder. He read prolifically and silently in his cushioned chair. He smoked incessantly and coughed noisily just about everywhere. I used to buy him a carton of Philip Morris every Father's Day, slaying a part of him with that gift of love. He laughed a lot; he had ulcers.

Yes, there's more I do recall and much more I don't. All that doesn't matter. What matters is that I have not tried too hard to enhance or destroy what has become an imposing but enigmatic family figure. Ancestor worship becomes a kind of conditioned reflex that jerks the descendant selves to death. He lives indelibly in my genes; he doesn't live imperiously in my recollection.

I know my father will remain a myth—as so many fathers do—less the man, perhaps, than his children and grandchildren suppose him to have been. And that is not a bad thing. I hope it is that way, rather than the reverse, with my own two children and me.

As for the real memory of my father, it serves me best by encouraging me to be an unabashedly loving father. I would wish that for all living fathers on their day and for their children every day.

49

Some Lives Go On

Previously unpublished—written in July, 1989

This article was never published. It was sent to The New York Times. *The person who returned it (not my usual editor, Frank Litsky) had three explanations in an accompanying note.*

1. *An apology for "losing it" on her desk, making it, when she 'found' it, no longer timely.*
2. *An explanation that the Times had already published a previous article "on the same subject." (I knew about this article—and referred to it in my piece. It was not "the same.")*
3. *She (the editor) was "saving me" for a more important subject (unnamed and never again mentioned).*

So I decided to include the article in this book for my own three reasons.

1. *I felt it to be an important topic at the time—and still do.*
2. *I thought it had been treated in an undeservedly cavalier fashion.*
3. *Because I can.*

The article was provoked by a suicide. Many pointed to a specific moment—a singular pitch—as the provocation for the act. That was not the thrust of this piece. I did not believe there was one causal factor—but I did believe that the player's act required a deeper examination—and proactive programs to help pre-empt such acts by other players in the future.

The insights provided by Rick Wolff in his article "What Happens When the Cheering Stops?" (*NY Times*, April. 23, 1989) were dramatically punctuated by the recent suicide of former major league pitcher, Donnie Moore.

One of Wolff's major concerns was that professional sports organizations have failed to actively acknowledge the lives the athletes must face once their athletic careers have ended. Such acknowledgement is prerequisite to the assistance that should be offered the athlete in facing and coping with a new life—and a 'new' self, at that. This is a responsibility that the best business corporations have come to understand and vigorously address.

Wolff's words were bright and true. How unfortunate that, as Emily Dickinson wrote, "... the truth must dazzle gradually / Or every man be blind." Perhaps the tragedy of Donnie Moore will shade the eyes of those who have the power to initiate programs for professional athletes.

Though the specific causes(s) of Moore's despondency can only be conjectured upon, some facts are known. Fact number one: He was affected to some degree by the pitch he threw to Dave Henderson in the 1986 American League Championship Series. One strike away from defeating Boston in that series, Moore, pitching with a tender/sore shoulder, threw a hanging forkball that Henderson hit over the left-centerfield fence. The home run tied the game that was eventually lost by Moore's California team to the Red Sox, who went on to the World Series.

Opinions obey the same laws as pendulums. Former California teammate Brian Downing expressed his view of the circumstance that led to Moore's suicide: "Everything revolved around one pitch." Downing then accused the sports writers of having "destroyed a man's life over one pitch. The guy was just not the same after that," Downing said.

Swinging from the opposite direction was Ralph Branca, who has worn his notoriety on his sleeve—the sleeve that covers the right arm that threw the pitch in 1951 to Bobby Thomson of the New York Giants. Thomson's 'shot heard round the world' went into the left field stands of the Polo Grounds and turned an impending Giants defeat into victory over the Brooklyn Dodgers—and a place in the World Series.

Branca, a successful businessman who has lived with a pitch etched deeper into baseball history than the one Moore threw, can't believe Henderson's homer could have been the catalyst for Moore's taking his life. "I cannot visualize being that depressed," Branca said. "I threw a home run pitch. So what? We lost ... Life goes on." Pictures of Branca at his locker after the game indicate a depressed player—*at that time.*

But lives go on. Or, at least, they should. However, they go on in a variety of ways. The quality of former professional athletes' lives is directly linked to their preparedness for living those lives. Self-awareness, perspective and coping mechanisms are more at issue than home-run pitches.

Montreal outfielder Hubie Brooks, a distant cousin of Moore, said, "The damage is done. Why point fingers? The real question is, "If that's the reason (for Moore's shooting himself and his wife—she survived) what does it say? What does it mean?" These are questions professional sports management must ask themselves and each other.

Fact number two: Donnie Moore, released by the Angels in 1988, was troubled by physical injuries, financial difficulties (despite have been highly salaried in the latter years of his career) and a failed marriage. He had attempted a comeback with the Kansas City Royals' Triple-A affiliate in Omaha. This failed also; the team had released him just over a month ago.

Moore's seventeen-year-old daughter, Demetria, offered this opinion: "When he got cut (by Omaha), he'd been really depressed about that. And then, I mean, here he is, the high-life career was off and then all of a sudden—boom—it's gone. And then he comes back to home ... and the marriage, the family, is all destroyed. What else does he have left?"

Another important question.

Chicago Cubs broadcaster Steve Stone, Moore's teammate on the 1975 Cubs, had this to say: "There are some personal demons that haunt all of us, and a lot of people are able to resign themselves to a life after baseball. But there are a lot of people who feel uncomfortable when the dream ends. In some players' minds, it ends a little too soon. I can't possibly try to interpret the motivations and what brought Donnie Moore to his decision to end his life, but I would have thought it had to be something outside of just the fact that he couldn't throw the baseball any longer."

And so the perspectives and motivations of others are interpreted freely. We all have our opinions; we all have our points of view. But look at the conjoining agents of Moore's despondency: self-identity, financial concerns, marriage and family relationships. We *all* deal with these issues on a daily basis, with varying degrees of success. Yet a professional athlete must, in addition to these issues, confront the broader problem of eventually making a transition into a new life—one he is often (usually?) not prepared to face or manage. It should be the responsibility of every professional sports organization to add to its agenda the on-going preparation of and counseling for these athletes—for their world in sport as they compete, and for their world after sport, as they live on.

There are many difficulties that the pro athlete has been sheltered from since his youth. As a rule, his specific precocity has been responsible for his general naïveté. His family and coaches often share the responsibility—the blame. Most athletes are not even aware of the problems they will face as professionals, let alone know what solutions or coping strategies to employ.

Their lives as professionals and former professionals would be greatly enhanced if their organizations helped prepare for their current and future lives. Some organizations *have* begun to understand. These few have initiated such programs, which help their players to:

Confront and understand the media

Become acquainted with skills for communicating with teammates and staff
    members

Seek sound financial advice
Be responsible family members
Initiate or continue further education
Consider and develop plans for a future career
Become familiar with performance enhancement approaches and stress management techniques
Develop proper habits of nutrition, rest and personal health care.

Commissioner A. Bartlett Giamatti has been in the process of implementing a broad program for Organized Baseball. When he was President of the National League, he formed a 'Player Personal Development Committee.' He is broadening its base. It is the Commissioner's conviction, shared by "virtually everyone" he has spoken with in baseball, "that we have some clear moral obligation to employees who are ballplayers."

The benefits of this plan should now be as clear as the moral obligation. But the problem of such a broad program of counseling is that it is essentially voluntary. The many players who believe their lives and responsibilities—their baseball worlds—are exclusive to any other concerns are those individuals who need the program most, and who are least likely to make an effort to avail themselves of it. American League President Bobby Brown has been frustrated by these players' lack of initiative.

The implication is apparent. Each organization—each *team*—must take the responsibility their athletes are either unaware of or unwilling to take. That lack of awareness and/or responsibility becomes part of the professional athlete's general problem.

When the athlete is 'brought to school' by a concerned employer he is quite often appreciative and, more significantly, receptive and responsive. More teams are examining ways of addressing their players' need on and of the field. (The Oakland Athletics, for whom I work, have had an extensive program in place since 1984.)

The word was sounded by Rick Wolff, Commissioner Giammati and numerous others. And now, Donnie Moore's final act has struck the same note with a sad clarity and a singular force.

Deeds, we must remember, are always more profound than words.

Postscript—Since this piece was written, many, if not all baseball organizations, have developed counseling programs. Drug and alcohol issues, personal mental health issues, family and financial matters have come under the umbrella of an industry-wide Employees Assistance Program. In addition, teams have hired sports psychologists and clinical psychologists to address players' on-field and off-field issues.

Recently, there was a breakthrough regarding the stigma of receiving such intervention. The mental health issues of three major league players, in particular, became public. Zach Greinke left his Kansas City team because of personal problems, received counseling, came back to play the following year—and won the Cy Young award. Joey Vott, the first baseman of the Cincinnati Reds, was put on the disabled list after the death of his father and a debilitating despondency, left the team, received counseling, returned—and as I write this, is a candidate for the league's Most Valuable Player award, 2010. Pitcher Ian Snell has spoken publicly about the intervention that 'saved his life.'

   Progress comes slowly, too late for some.

50

Late Shot

The Los Angeles Times, October 3, 2001

Twenty-five years before this article appeared in the L.A. Times, *it was published in* The Rutland Herald. *In 1976, it commemorated the 25th anniversary of the event treated in the article; 1981 was the 50th anniversary. A few additions were made—mostly based on information that came my way during that interim period. The assistant editor at the* L.A. Times *was very interested in the slant of this article, since it focused more on the defeated Dodgers than the victorious Giants.*

The story's 'tragic hero' was a fine man, a man I wanted to meet and offer an opportunity to explain what I thought was an injustice done to him years before.

I packed my wife and two children into a rented Winnebago—and off we went on a summer vacation trip. But first, a stop at the Waldoboro, Maine, home of Clyde Sukeforth.

Today is the 50th anniversary of one of the most dramatic baseball moments in one of the most historic games. Old-time Giants fan recall it with a nostalgic titillation. Bobby Thomson's ninth-inning home run, hit off Ralph Branca on October 3, 1951. The so-called Miracle of Coogan's Bluff. "The Shot Heard Round the World." A debilitating shot to the heart of old-time Dodger fans.

With it, the New York Giants defeated the Brooklyn Dodgers in the final game of a three-game playoff for the National League pennant.

Clyde Sukeforth was the Dodgers' bullpen coach, and it was he who reputedly "chose" to send Branca into that now historic game. Sukeforth hadn't talked much about the game afterward, but, really, he rarely talked much about anything. In the summer of 1976, however, the reticent, stereotypical New Englander allowed me to "come on ahead" from my Vermont home for a visit with him. I'd explained that I wanted to talk about that "shot'—about that game—since we were closing in on its 25th anniversary.

"I also heard a little something I wanted to run by you," I said during our phone conversation.

He asked, "What might that be?"

I glanced down at a line I'd written in my notes. "The past may be seemingly irrevocable," I recited. "But truth itself has no deadline."

His response was barely audible: "I guess we can have a little chat."

The morning vapors enveloping Back Cove in Waldoboro, Maine, lifted slowly and indifferently. Driving cautiously around a bend, I fancied myself moving through a haze of impressions, trying to navigate toward some historical clarity.

What soon became visible was a small house nestled in a rocky and solitary corner. The man of the house had already been up and out—out after bird on the wing, his Brittany spaniel at his side. He was returning to the house as I arrived. He greeted me. We went into the house; his wife greeted each of us with a steaming cup of coffee. "Let's chat," he said, pointing to where he wanted me to sit.

Clyde Sukeforth had been a man for many seasons. A right-hand man in Brooklyn for baseball's legendary Mahatma, Branch Rickey, Sukeforth became a trusted scout, coach and emissary. It was Sukeforth who made the initial personal contacts with Jackie Robinson when the sport's color line was broken. It was Sukeforth who accompanied Rickey to Pittsburgh in later years, and who was instrumental in procuring that city's immortal, Roberto Clemente.

And it was Sukeforth at whom Dodger manager Charley Dressen directed the heat for sending Branca into the game. Sukeforth took the heat, and he never disputed, never disavowed what eventually became history, the proverbial fable agreed upon.

He wore his age remarkably, even into his 90's. He wore his memories comfortably, like a favorite fishing hat.

Let's set the stage for his recollections.

On August 12, 1951, the Dodgers held a commanding 13 ½-game lead over their hated archrivals, the Giants, who had opened the season ignominiously by losing their first 11 games.

On that August day, however, the Giants began an astounding reversal by recording the first of 16 consecutive victories. New York manager Leo Durocher—a former Dodger manager—and his 20-year-old rookie wonder, Willie Mays, inspired them to 39 victories in the final 47 games. The Giants climbed into a first-place tie with Brooklyn by winning their last seven regular-season games.

The Dodgers, meanwhile, played with their eyes over their shoulders, their bats under the ball and their butts scraping the ground. And they were forced into a three-game playoff with the Giants to determine the pennant winner.

The first two games were split, and the stage was set for the dramatic finale. Hundreds of thousands have claimed witness to the event, but only 32,320 paid to sit in the Polo Grounds on that overcast October afternoon.

The Dodgers scored in the first inning. Pee Wee Reese and Duke Snider walked, and Robinson singled in a run.

Thomson doubled in the fifth for the Giants, and that had Branca stirring in the bullpen. Branca and Carl Erskine were warming up seriously by the seventh inning.

Brooklyn's starting pitcher, Don Newcombe, had complained to his catcher, Roy Campanella, and to Robinson. He claimed he had nothing left in his arm. In this most difficult and crucial game and situation, Robinson, as he typically did, asserted himself.

"Go out there and pitch until your #%^*# arm falls off," he's said to have commanded.

Newcombe responded, and through the eighth the Dodgers had built their lead to 4-1. Brooklyn did not score in the top of the ninth. The Giants, in their last turn at bat, were faced with the prospect of having their gallant August-September heroics blown from Coogan's Bluff into the Harlem River.

"Well," Sukeforth began, "it was quite an inning. We were leading, 4-1. Alvin Dark led off the ninth for them and hit a little ball to the right side that just managed to be a single. Don Mueller, a lefty, hits to the same place and the ball goes into right field. Men on first and second.

"Funny thing, nobody's ever found out why (Gil) Hodges was holding the runner on close at first base with Mueller up. Dark wasn't going to steal in that situation—and even if he did, it wouldn't matter. Mueller's ball would have been handled if Hodges was in normal position. I'm surprised Gilly didn't think of that without Dressen."

As a footnote, after a thoughtful pause, Sukeforth added, "A little thing like that meant a lot."

Was this a subtle "payback shot" from Sukeforth? Dressen, the Dodgers egotistical manager, was known to have told his teams, "Just stay close; I'll think of something." He apparently didn't think of moving Hodges.

Former big league manager Dick Williams was a player on the Brooklyn bench that fateful day. He and other Dodgers—Robinson, Reese and Snider, most notably—had seen what they thought was a manager losing control in a big game.

"By losing control of himself ... he lost control of the team," Williams said.

Robinson had shouted in the dugout for someone to tell Dressen to stop pacing, he was making everyone else edgy.

Sukeforth had noticed Dressen's edginess as well.

"He started calling (the bullpen) in the eighth inning and kept right on into the ninth," Sukeforth recalled. "He sounded frantic. 'Who's ready? Who's ready?' He'd always have a plan for who would relieve, when he would come in, if such-and-such happened, and so on. Not that day.

"Well now, out he comes to talk to the fella pitching (Newcombe). He talked to him and went back to the dugout. Monte Irvin then popped up to Gilly. One out.

"But (Whitey) Lockman doubles to left; Dark scores, Mueller goes to third. He hurt himself sliding, remember, and was carried off the field. Hartung—remember that name?—Clint Hartung ran for him. So it's 4-2, men on second and third. Bobby Thomson was up next. Branca was ready in the bullpen, so Dressen calls him in to pitch. The rest everybody remembers."

"Not everybody," I said. "Anyhow, I'd like you to take your account to the very end."

Sukeforth's tone was bittersweet, his account succinct: "Well, it was just a 260-foot home run."

Actually, it was measured at 320 feet. In any case, somewhere in the inviting left-field stands of the Polo Grounds, a National League ball landed. Branca had thrown it; Thomson had hit it. The world has talked about the 'shot.' And baseball historians have revered the moment. The Giants won the game, 5-4, and with it, baseball's most spectacular pennant race.

But the matter does not—did not—end there. After the abrupt and painful loss, Dressen was asked a number of direct and difficult questions by sportswriters. An acknowledged, if not beloved, baseball tactician, he had an understandably tough time of it.

But he never had been known as a possessor of grace under spotlight. Rather, he could claim some infamy for self-praise in high moments and buck passing in low ones. Someone once made the claim that Dressen's ego could fill an otherwise empty ballpark.

One writer asked, "Why did you bring Branca in to pitch?"

The buck was presented.

Dressen's response: "Sukeforth said he was ready."

The buck was passed, and it has been in Sukeforth's pocket ever since.

Forty-nine years later, George Will, in the Dec. 25, 2000, issue of *Newsweek* ("Y2K—You Must Remember This"), closed his column by "reminding" readers: "...Sukeforth answered the Polo Grounds bullpen phone and recommended that Ralph Branca, rather than Carl Erskine, pitch to Bobby Thomson. Oh, well."

Oh well, indeed.

A German proverb says, "Justice is a nose of wax." On that summer morning in 1976, I encouraged Clyde Sukeforth to twitch his Alsatian nose.

"Shoot," he said, smiling again, "that answer never really bothered me. Charley did things like that sometimes. It doesn't matter. Everybody knows the manager is responsible for decisions. But I'll tell you something amusing." He meant: the real story. This smile was less benign than the previous one.

"Branca started loosening up earlier in the game, never thinking he'd be pitching that day. He was hoping to be picked as the starting pitcher in the first game of the World Series, against the Yankees. So he was firing that ball after a while—showing off, you might say—probably thinking I'd tell Dressen how good he was throwing and give him a recommendation.

"Then when the trouble starts to develop in the game. Erskine gets up. Now, everyone knew that Erskine was troubled by arm problems. Sometimes he was OK, but sometimes he could hardly throw the ball. That day he couldn't even reach the catcher with some of his warmup pitches. Here's Branca poppin' and Erskine the way he was. Branca was the only one who could come in when that big guy (Newcombe) couldn't go any further."

He paused and said, without expression in his face or voice, "It didn't matter what anybody said, he was the only one."

Oh well, this *final* 'shot' is not meant to resound 'round the world.' On this momentous baseball anniversary it barely qualifies as a shot. Still justice should also be the right of the silent.

In this case, the right of Clyde Sukeforth—a constant man, a faithful Dodger—who died in that little Maine cove last year. He was 98 years old.

About the Author

Harvey Dorfman's background was in education and psychology, as a teacher, counselor, coach and consultant. He was a goalie on his college's national championship soccer team, and the coach of a high school state championship basketball team.

In 1984 he developed and implemented a sport psychology program for the Oakland Athletics baseball team, working full-time as an instructor/counselor. He left Oakland in 1994, to work for the Florida Marlins, and was with them through their '97 championship season. The following year he worked for the expansion Tampa Bay Devil Rays.

Dorfman worked with two professional hockey teams, the Vancouver Canucks and the New York Islanders, and consulted for the Calgary Flames and the Washington Capitals.

His freelance work in sport psychology included work with a professional female bowler, a golfer on the professional senior tour, an Eclipse Award-winning jockey, a professional tennis player, an Olympic skier and an NFL quarterback. He also worked with a singer with the San Francisco Opera Company.

In 1999, Dorfman became a full-time consultant in sport psychology and staff development for the Scott Boras Corporation, an agency that represents professional baseball players.

He wrote, with Karl Kuehl, *The Mental Game of Baseball*. He also wrote *The Mental ABC's of Pitching*, *The Mental Keys to Hitting* and *Coaching the Mental Game*.

Each Branch, Each Needle, published in 2010, was the final volume in a trilogy of anecdotal memoirs. The first, *Persuasion of My Days*, was published in 2005. *Copying It Down*, the second, was published in 2009.

Dorfman was also for many years a freelance journalist, with work appearing in *The New York Times*, *Boston Globe*, and *Los Angeles Times*, among others. While teaching in Vermont, he wrote a weekly column entitled "Miscellany" for the *Rutland Herald*. More recently, his "Mind Game" column appeared in *PRO*, a quarterly magazine for professional athletes. He lectured at major universities and for corporations on psychology, self-enhancement, management strategies and leadership training.

He was the subject of feature articles in such publications as *GQ* and *Men's Journal* and was a frequent guest on satellite radio and ESPN sports programming.

Dorfman was inducted in the Burr & Burton Academy Hall of Fame as a coach in 2008. In 2003, he was elected to the SUNY-Brockport Alumni Association's Hall of Heritage. In 2005, on the 50th anniversary of the school's championship soccer season, he was inducted with his teammates into the Golden Eagle Hall of Fame. He was inducted into this Hall as an individual in 2010.

He continued to counsel and write up to the time of his death at age 75 in 2011, shortly after his compilation of the articles in this book.

www.ingramcontent.com/pod-product-compliance
Lightning Source LLC
Chambersburg PA
CBHW071518100726
47908CB00004B/1210